THE RISE OF ISLAM

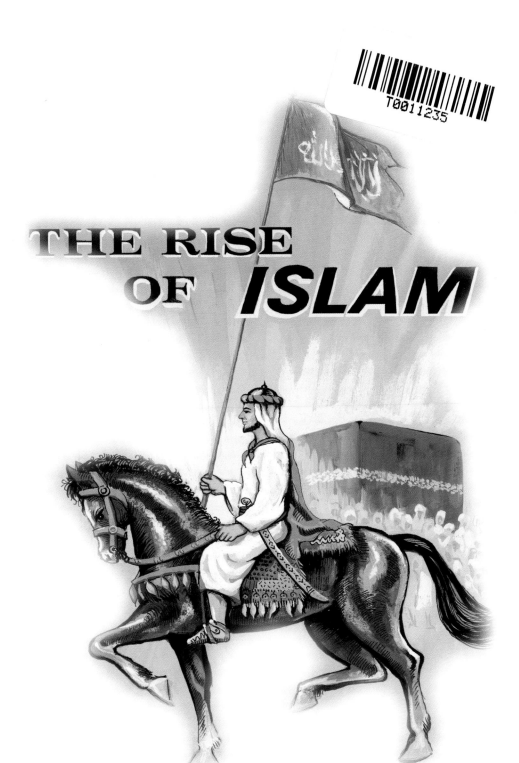

The Rise of Islam: History of Islam - Illustrated

First Published in 1970 The Muslim Assembly
(Cape Town, South Africa)

Published in 2022 by THE ISLAMIC FOUNDATION, UK.

Distributed by
KUBE PUBLISHING LTD
MCC, Ratby Lane
Markfield, Leicesterhsire, LE67 9SY
Tel: +44 (0)1530 249230
Email: info@kubepublishing.com
Website: www.kubepublishing.com

Author: Arshad Gamiet
Editor: Mogamat T Ajam

A Catalogue-in-Publication Data record for this book is available fro, the British Library

ISBN: 978-0-86037-816-7
EISBN: 978-0-86037-821-1

Printed in Turkey by Elma Basim

Author's note, 2021

I would like to thank Haris Ahmad of Kube Publishing, for offering to reprint this book. Haris' father brought him a copy when he was a young boy. His father is the eminent scholar, Prof. Khurshid Ahmad. How this book came into their hands is another story. Allah works in the most mysterious ways...

Our lives appear to be a random mix of jigsaw puzzle pieces that have no connection with each other. In the fullness of time, we see Allah's master plan emerging out of apparently disconnected events.

In the summer of 1967 I was a curious 21 year old, walking home from lectures. This was my final year at the University of Cape Town's Michaelis School of Fine Art. On my way, I would meet my friend, Mr Halim, who owned a corner shop in District Six. Here we would share a chilled Pepsi and a chat. Just inside the front door stood racks of English and Afrikaans newspapers, magazines and picture-story books ('foto- romans,' Afrikaans for 'photo-romance') paperbacks. South Africa had no television yet, so those books were like printed equivalents of soap operas of the day.

Whilst Mr Halim and I discussed the latest news, I noted how quickly the picture story books were being snapped up off the shelves, much quicker than the newspapers. Women rushing home from work in the textile factories would drop in to buy the latest ones, without even glancing at the newspapers. That made a lot of sense to me. These women experience hardship and humiliation daily. Why bother to read about the grim life in Apartheid South Africa, when the fantasy world of perfect love and romance in picture story books was so much more appealing?

If only these long suffering people could find something more substantial, more life- affirming and enriching than mere escapism, I wondered. If only they could read some really inspiring books to extend their mental and spiritual horizons...

I remembered my own love for the picture-story genre that began much earlier: the 'Boys Own' classics; the Biggles books; the gutsy, all-conquering World War II heroes with their Spitfires, Messerschmitts and Hurricanes. But there was one picture story that endured in a class of its own. It brings back fond memories of my early childhood: Prince Valiant, by Hal Foster. It was always there, in glorious Technicolor, on the last page of the Sunday Times comic supplement. Even as a 10 year old, I used to relish the artwork, the keen attention to detail, the costumes, the weaponry, the drawings so meticulously crafted: a sheer joy to behold.

That's where I found the idea and the inspiration for this book. Why not tell the beautiful story about how Islam began, by using Prince Valliant – style pictures? I had no pretensions about this. I was no Hal Foster, and I had no King Features Syndicate to back me. Colour printing would be prohibitively expensive. But why not just do it in plain black and white?

It is now 53 years since that day in June, 1967, when I started planning, writing and drawing The Rise of Islam. Bit by bit over the following months the book took shape. But about halfway through, I stopped abruptly. An unexpected opportunity had come my way...

The Vice-Chancellor of Karachi University in Pakistan, Dr Ishtiaq Hussain Qureshi was on a lecture tour of South Africa. I was asked to join his reception committee as Chairman of the University of Cape Town Islamic Association. It was my job to offer a welcome speech in the City Hall. Noticing my youthful enthusiasm, Dr Qureshi invited me to spend a year at his university for a short course on Islam. A generous businessman, Haji Aziez Gool, sponsored my trip. I later found that Haji Aziez was quietly sponsoring many other students who were studying abroad.

1968 was my year for studying and travelling in Pakistan, Afghanistan and Iran. That's also when I met Prof Khurshid Ahmad, who taught me Economics at Karachi University. When I returned home to Cape Town, it was back to job-hunting again.

In apartheid South Africa, good jobs were scarce for people of colour like me. My efforts were rewarded by a brief spell as a Display Artist for Cuthbert's Shoes, followed by an offer from the Muslim Assembly (Cape). They needed someone with audio-visual skills to produce teaching aids for schools and community centres. Under the expert tutelage of my dear friend and mentor, Dr Cassiem Dharsey, I enjoyed two of the most creative years of my working life. That dusty portfolio for The Rise of Islam was re-opened and, with the backing of the Muslim Assembly and strong encouragement from its late Chairman, Dr H M Kotwal, this book was completed on 25th May, 1970. The original print run of 10,000 copies was sold out within a year.

Eight years after my trip to Pakistan, quite unexpectedly, I received a letter from Prof Khurshid Ahmad. He was now based in Leicester, UK, having set up the Islamic Foundation there. He had found a copy of my book in the foyer of an Islamic Foreign Ministers' conference in Tripoli, Libya, in 1976. How my book got there, I have absolutely no idea. We exchanged letters and I told him that my wife and I were about to migrate to Australia with our two sons, and I was keen to write and illustrate more children's books. Prof Khurshid invited me over to see what the Islamic Foundation was doing, and offered me a job there. So it was good bye, Australia and hello, UK...

I'm so grateful to Prof Khurshid Ahmad for inviting me to work at the Islamic Foundation where I enjoyed 3 happy years, 42 years ago. I'm grateful to his son, Haris, for reprinting my book. It has been out of print for 50 years. Mostly, I'm grateful to Allah for helping to turn a young man's idea into a useful and inspiring story book. I'm truly amazed that seemingly disconnected events in my life have come together in such a remarkable way. Eight years after meeting Prof Khurshid in Pakistan, this book caught his attention in Libya, inspired him to write to me in South Africa, changed my plans of migrating to Australia and got me a job in Britain. I made plans, but Allah is truly the best of planners!

Dear reader: If you enjoy this book as much as I enjoyed writing and illustrating it, remember that all praise is due to Allah alone. Any faults you may find are mine entirely. I ask you to remember us all in your prayers: for your Muslim brothers and sisters at Kube Publishing, at the Islamic Foundation in Leicester and Muslim Assembly in Cape Town, past and present, and for me and my family.

As-salaamu'alaykum. Peace be with you

Arshad Gamiet.
Buckinghamshire, UK. 24th September 2020. 7 Safar 1442 AH

Foreword

In the Name of Allah, The Merciful and Compassionate !

The aim of this work is to present to the public, and especially the children, an idea of how one of the world's great religions, Islam, came into existence.

This is a new and bold attempt to take the reader into a period of man's eventful past. It tells a beautiful story in picture form to aid our understanding and it is a job done with reverence and sensitivity. In every page pictures have been a universal language for telling a story. A Chinese proverb says, "A picture is better than a thousand words". Pictures convey a much more real and concrete impression than words alone can do.

For this reason the author has used this manner to relate for our benefit an inspiring story. If the reader has gained a better understanding and has been inspired to read more or lead a purposeful life, then the author's hopes are realised.

The face and form of the main person in this story are (in accordance with Muslim practice) not portrayed. His face and form are not as of great importance as the manner in which his teachings and examples have changed the world. Humanity at large was granted a purposeful life, a new faith, a new society and a new culture by the advent of Muhammad (May peace and blessings be upon him). In the following pages we shall see how this glorious miracle was accomplished.

We pray that this book achieves its purpose. May it be judged according to the expressed intention of the author.

M. Aja

Editor
25th April, 1970

CHAPTER ONE:
Arabia and the Arabs

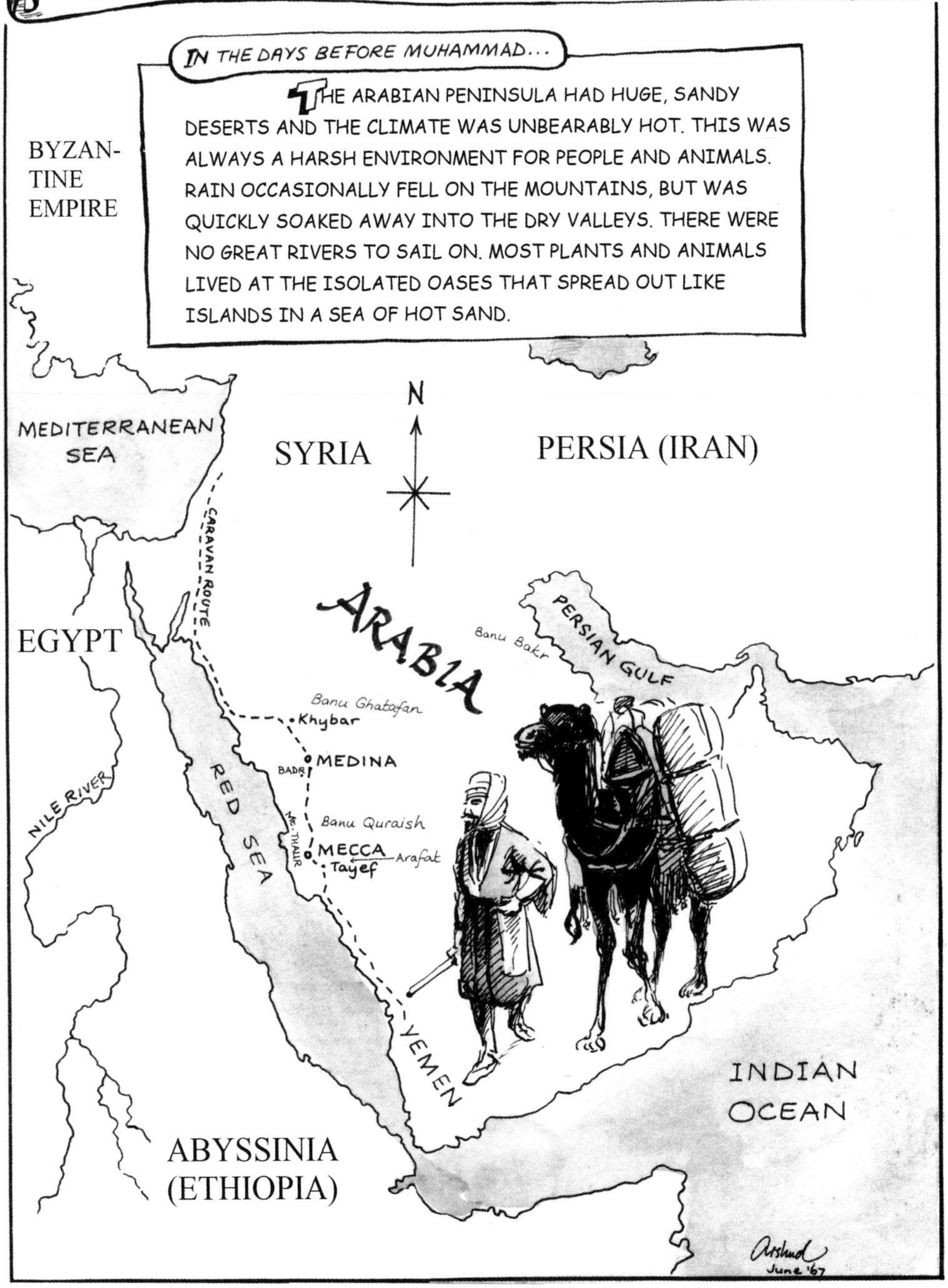
IN THE DAYS BEFORE MUHAMMAD...
THE ARABIAN PENINSULA HAD HUGE, SANDY DESERTS AND THE CLIMATE WAS UNBEARABLY HOT. THIS WAS ALWAYS A HARSH ENVIRONMENT FOR PEOPLE AND ANIMALS. RAIN OCCASIONALLY FELL ON THE MOUNTAINS, BUT WAS QUICKLY SOAKED AWAY INTO THE DRY VALLEYS. THERE WERE NO GREAT RIVERS TO SAIL ON. MOST PLANTS AND ANIMALS LIVED AT THE ISOLATED OASES THAT SPREAD OUT LIKE ISLANDS IN A SEA OF HOT SAND.
BYZANTINE EMPIRE
MEDITERRANEAN SEA
SYRIA
N
PERSIA (IRAN)
CARAVAN ROUTE
ARABIA
PERSIAN GULF
Banu Bakr
EGYPT
Banu Ghatafan
Khybar
MEDINA
BADR
RED SEA
NILE RIVER
Mt. THAUR
Banu Quraish
MECCA
Tayef
Arafat
YEMEN
INDIAN OCEAN
ABYSSINIA (ETHIOPIA)

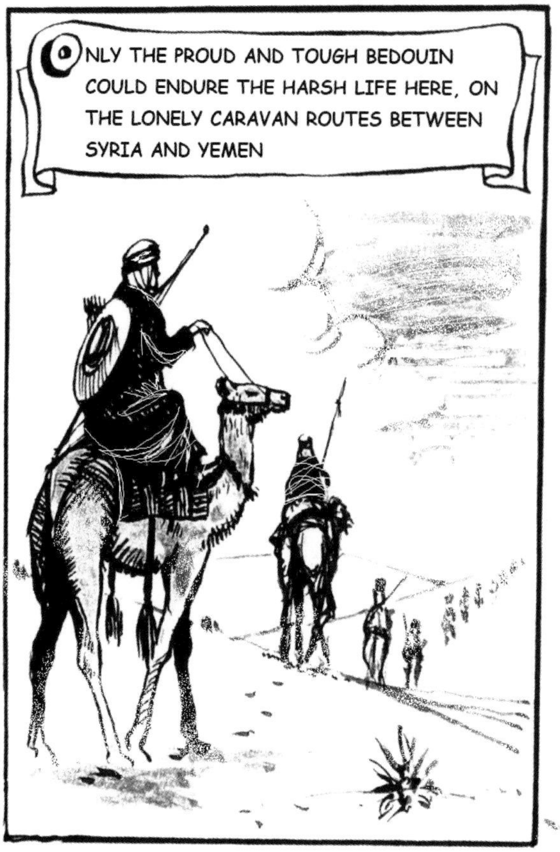
ONLY THE PROUD AND TOUGH BEDOUIN COULD ENDURE THE HARSH LIFE HERE, ON THE LONELY CARAVAN ROUTES BETWEEN SYRIA AND YEMEN

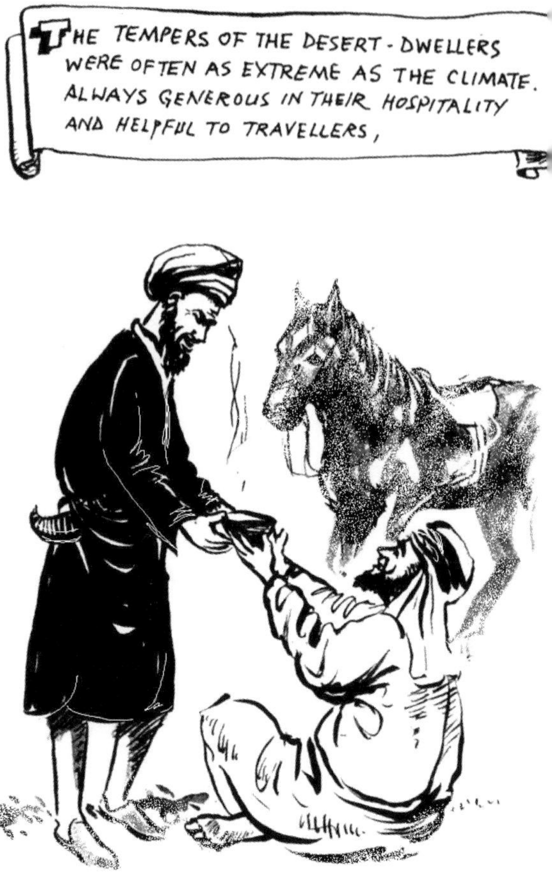
THE TEMPERS OF THE DESERT-DWELLERS WERE OFTEN AS EXTREME AS THE CLIMATE. ALWAYS GENEROUS IN THEIR HOSPITALITY AND HELPFUL TO TRAVELLERS,

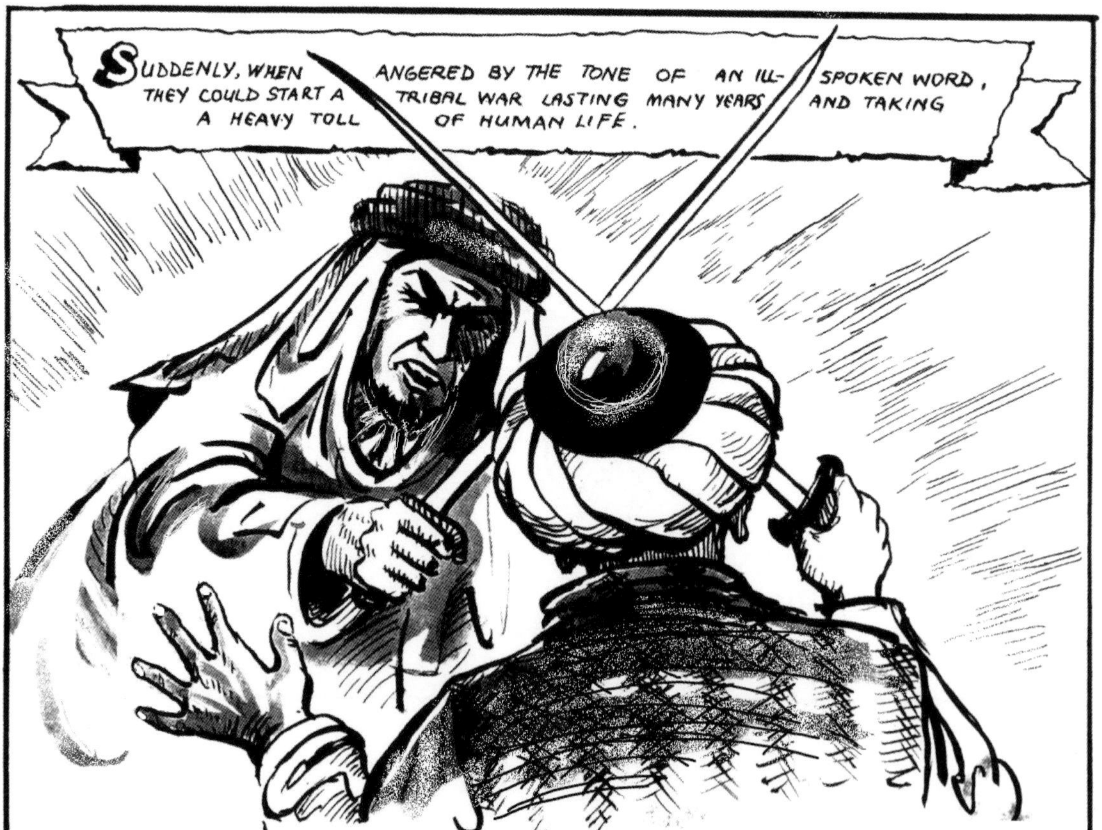
SUDDENLY, WHEN ANGERED BY THE TONE OF AN ILL-SPOKEN WORD, THEY COULD START A TRIBAL WAR LASTING MANY YEARS AND TAKING A HEAVY TOLL OF HUMAN LIFE.

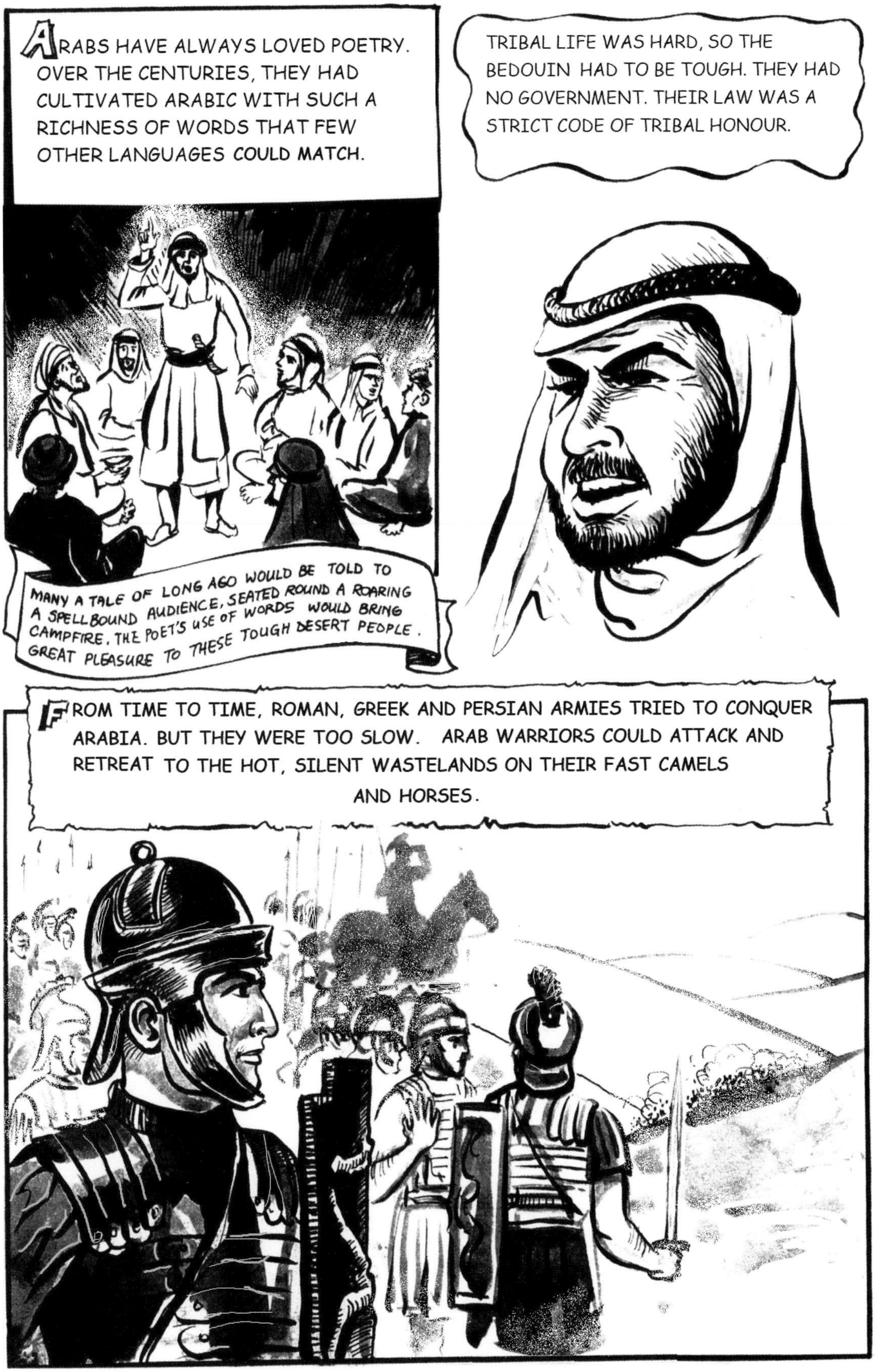
ARABS HAVE ALWAYS LOVED POETRY. OVER THE CENTURIES, THEY HAD CULTIVATED ARABIC WITH SUCH A RICHNESS OF WORDS THAT FEW OTHER LANGUAGES COULD MATCH.
TRIBAL LIFE WAS HARD, SO THE BEDOUIN HAD TO BE TOUGH. THEY HAD NO GOVERNMENT. THEIR LAW WAS A STRICT CODE OF TRIBAL HONOUR.
MANY A TALE OF LONG AGO WOULD BE TOLD TO A SPELLBOUND AUDIENCE, SEATED ROUND A ROARING CAMPFIRE. THE POET'S USE OF WORDS WOULD BRING GREAT PLEASURE TO THESE TOUGH DESERT PEOPLE.
FROM TIME TO TIME, ROMAN, GREEK AND PERSIAN ARMIES TRIED TO CONQUER ARABIA. BUT THEY WERE TOO SLOW. ARAB WARRIORS COULD ATTACK AND RETREAT TO THE HOT, SILENT WASTELANDS ON THEIR FAST CAMELS AND HORSES.

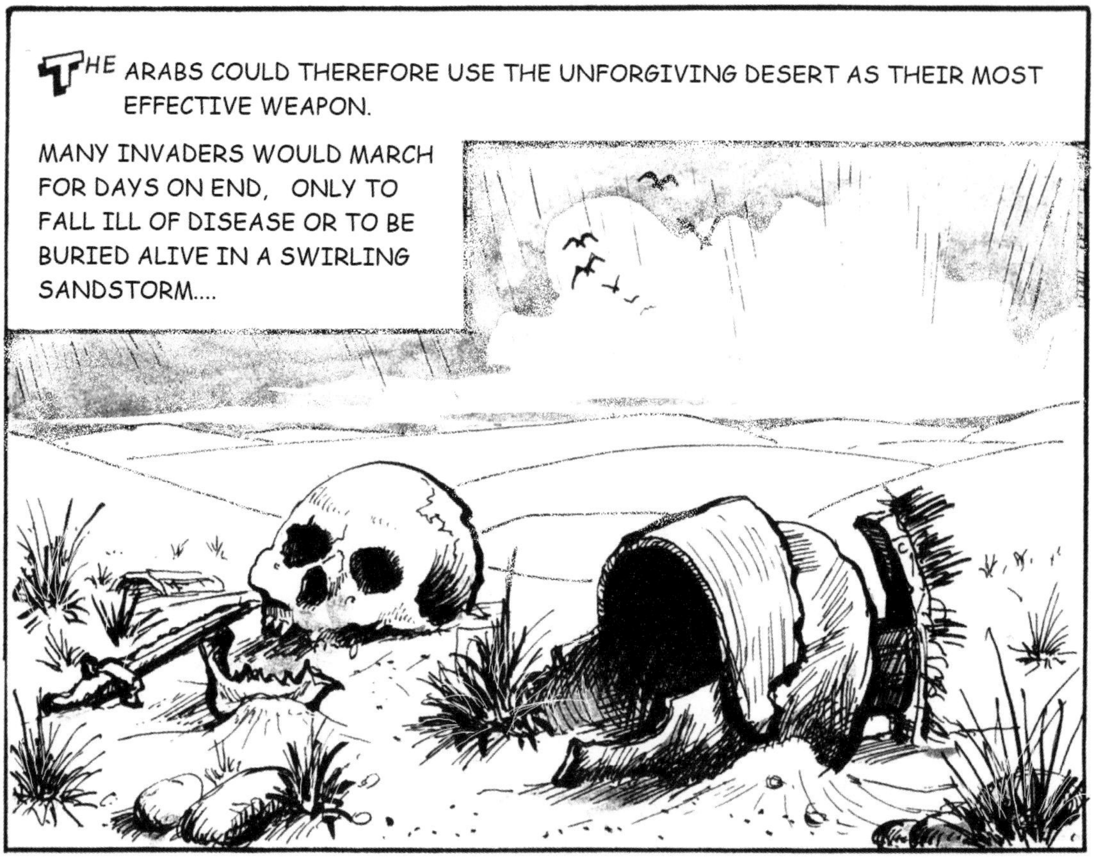
THE ARABS COULD THEREFORE USE THE UNFORGIVING DESERT AS THEIR MOST EFFECTIVE WEAPON.
MANY INVADERS WOULD MARCH FOR DAYS ON END, ONLY TO FALL ILL OF DISEASE OR TO BE BURIED ALIVE IN A SWIRLING SANDSTORM....

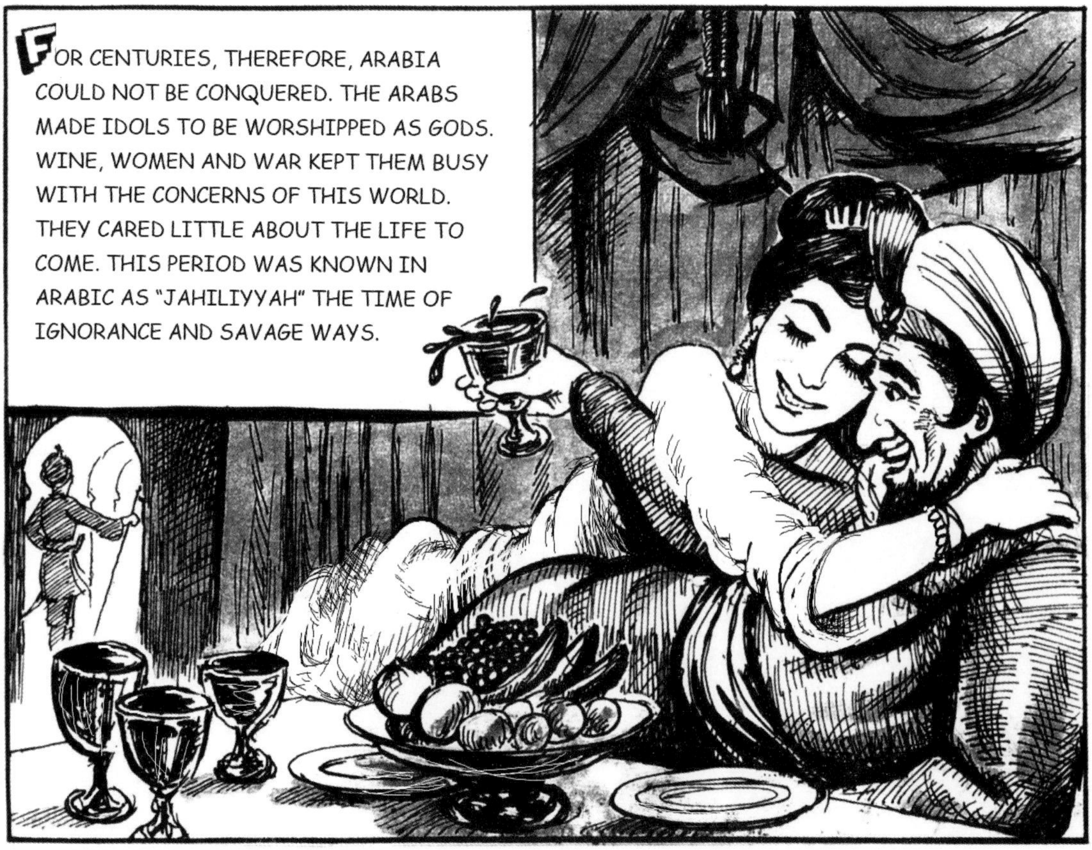
FOR CENTURIES, THEREFORE, ARABIA COULD NOT BE CONQUERED. THE ARABS MADE IDOLS TO BE WORSHIPPED AS GODS. WINE, WOMEN AND WAR KEPT THEM BUSY WITH THE CONCERNS OF THIS WORLD. THEY CARED LITTLE ABOUT THE LIFE TO COME. THIS PERIOD WAS KNOWN IN ARABIC AS "JAHILIYYAH" THE TIME OF IGNORANCE AND SAVAGE WAYS.

CHAPTER TWO:
The Coming of Muhammad

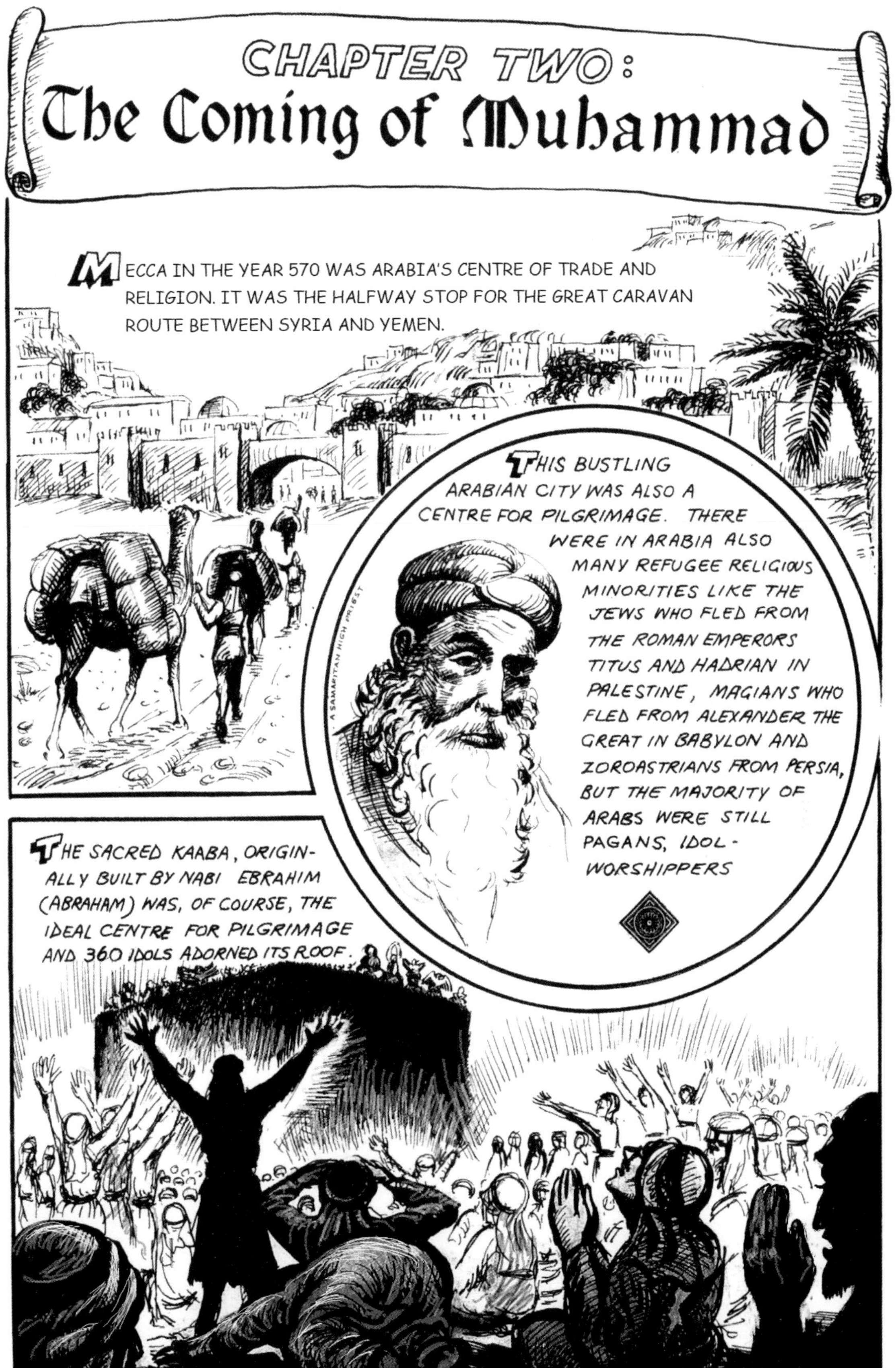
MECCA IN THE YEAR 570 WAS ARABIA'S CENTRE OF TRADE AND RELIGION. IT WAS THE HALFWAY STOP FOR THE GREAT CARAVAN ROUTE BETWEEN SYRIA AND YEMEN.
THIS BUSTLING ARABIAN CITY WAS ALSO A CENTRE FOR PILGRIMAGE. THERE WERE IN ARABIA ALSO MANY REFUGEE RELIGIOUS MINORITIES LIKE THE JEWS WHO FLED FROM THE ROMAN EMPERORS TITUS AND HADRIAN IN PALESTINE, MAGIANS WHO FLED FROM ALEXANDER THE GREAT IN BABYLON AND ZOROASTRIANS FROM PERSIA, BUT THE MAJORITY OF ARABS WERE STILL PAGANS, IDOL-WORSHIPPERS
A SAMARITAN HIGH PRIEST
THE SACRED KAABA, ORIGINALLY BUILT BY NABI EBRAHIM (ABRAHAM) WAS, OF COURSE, THE IDEAL CENTRE FOR PILGRIMAGE AND 360 IDOLS ADORNED ITS ROOF.

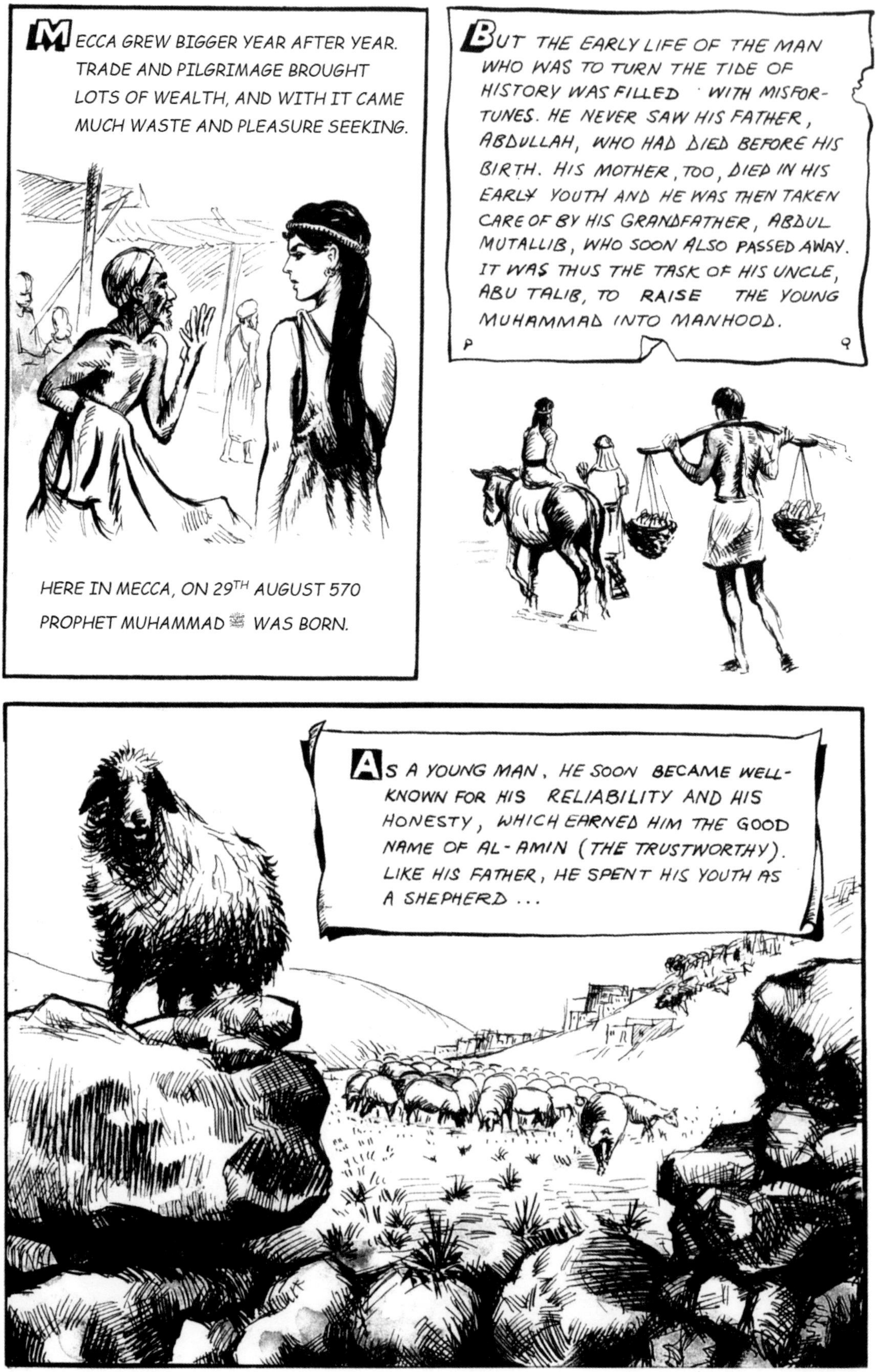
MECCA GREW BIGGER YEAR AFTER YEAR. TRADE AND PILGRIMAGE BROUGHT LOTS OF WEALTH, AND WITH IT CAME MUCH WASTE AND PLEASURE SEEKING.
HERE IN MECCA, ON 29TH AUGUST 570 PROPHET MUHAMMAD ﷺ WAS BORN.
BUT THE EARLY LIFE OF THE MAN WHO WAS TO TURN THE TIDE OF HISTORY WAS FILLED WITH MISFORTUNES. HE NEVER SAW HIS FATHER, ABDULLAH, WHO HAD DIED BEFORE HIS BIRTH. HIS MOTHER, TOO, DIED IN HIS EARLY YOUTH AND HE WAS THEN TAKEN CARE OF BY HIS GRANDFATHER, ABDUL MUTALLIB, WHO SOON ALSO PASSED AWAY. IT WAS THUS THE TASK OF HIS UNCLE, ABU TALIB, TO RAISE THE YOUNG MUHAMMAD INTO MANHOOD.
AS A YOUNG MAN, HE SOON BECAME WELL-KNOWN FOR HIS RELIABILITY AND HIS HONESTY, WHICH EARNED HIM THE GOOD NAME OF AL-AMIN (THE TRUSTWORTHY). LIKE HIS FATHER, HE SPENT HIS YOUTH AS A SHEPHERD ...

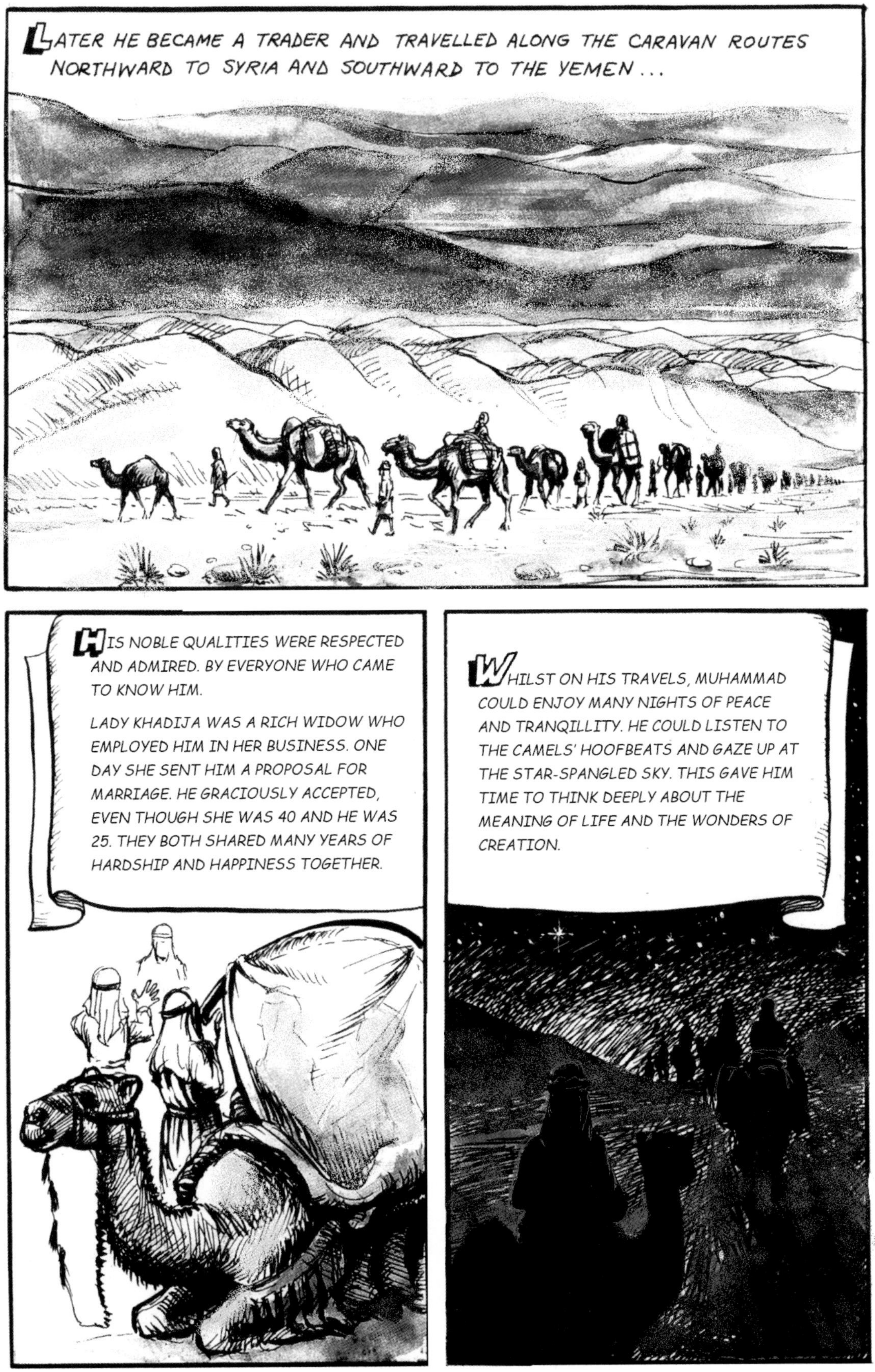
LATER HE BECAME A TRADER AND TRAVELLED ALONG THE CARAVAN ROUTES NORTHWARD TO SYRIA AND SOUTHWARD TO THE YEMEN ...
HIS NOBLE QUALITIES WERE RESPECTED AND ADMIRED. BY EVERYONE WHO CAME TO KNOW HIM.
LADY KHADIJA WAS A RICH WIDOW WHO EMPLOYED HIM IN HER BUSINESS. ONE DAY SHE SENT HIM A PROPOSAL FOR MARRIAGE. HE GRACIOUSLY ACCEPTED, EVEN THOUGH SHE WAS 40 AND HE WAS 25. THEY BOTH SHARED MANY YEARS OF HARDSHIP AND HAPPINESS TOGETHER.
WHILST ON HIS TRAVELS, MUHAMMAD COULD ENJOY MANY NIGHTS OF PEACE AND TRANQILLITY. HE COULD LISTEN TO THE CAMELS' HOOFBEATS AND GAZE UP AT THE STAR-SPANGLED SKY. THIS GAVE HIM TIME TO THINK DEEPLY ABOUT THE MEANING OF LIFE AND THE WONDERS OF CREATION.

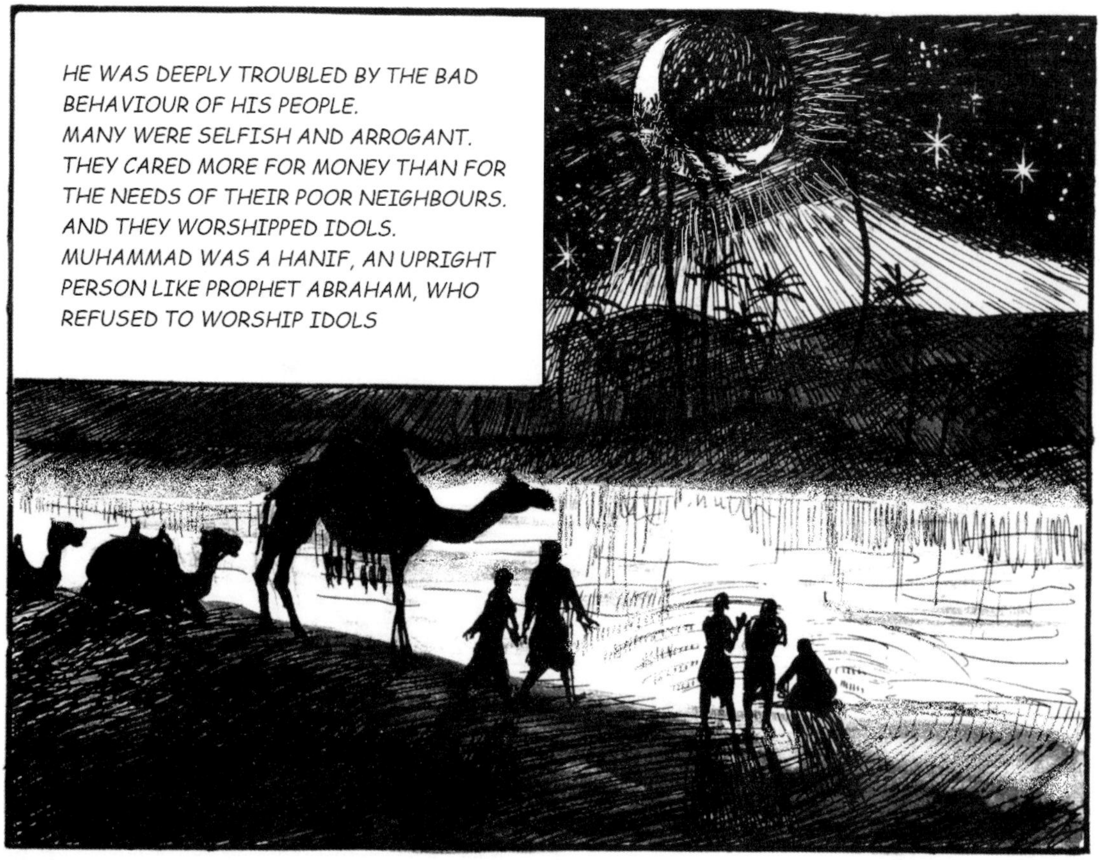
HE WAS DEEPLY TROUBLED BY THE BAD BEHAVIOUR OF HIS PEOPLE.
MANY WERE SELFISH AND ARROGANT.
THEY CARED MORE FOR MONEY THAN FOR THE NEEDS OF THEIR POOR NEIGHBOURS.
AND THEY WORSHIPPED IDOLS.
MUHAMMAD WAS A HANIF, AN UPRIGHT PERSON LIKE PROPHET ABRAHAM, WHO REFUSED TO WORSHIP IDOLS

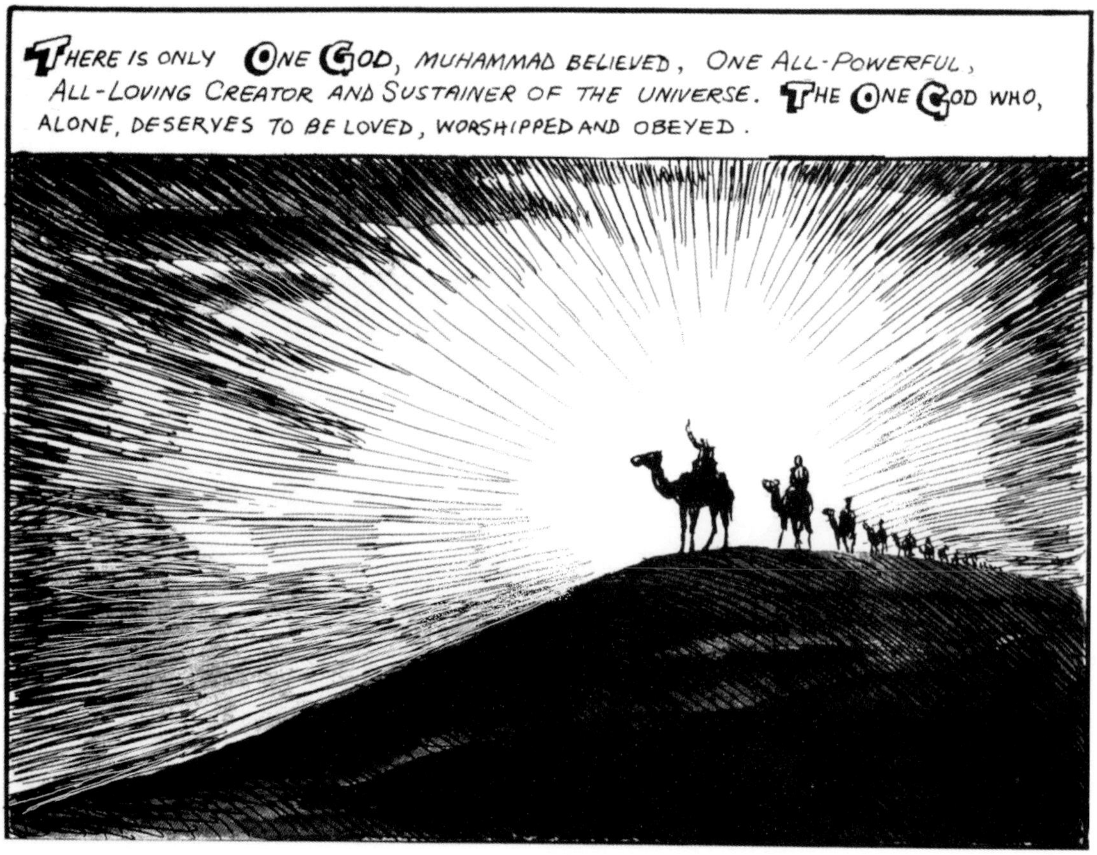
THERE IS ONLY ONE GOD, MUHAMMAD BELIEVED, ONE ALL-POWERFUL, ALL-LOVING CREATOR AND SUSTAINER OF THE UNIVERSE. THE ONE GOD WHO, ALONE, DESERVES TO BE LOVED, WORSHIPPED AND OBEYED.

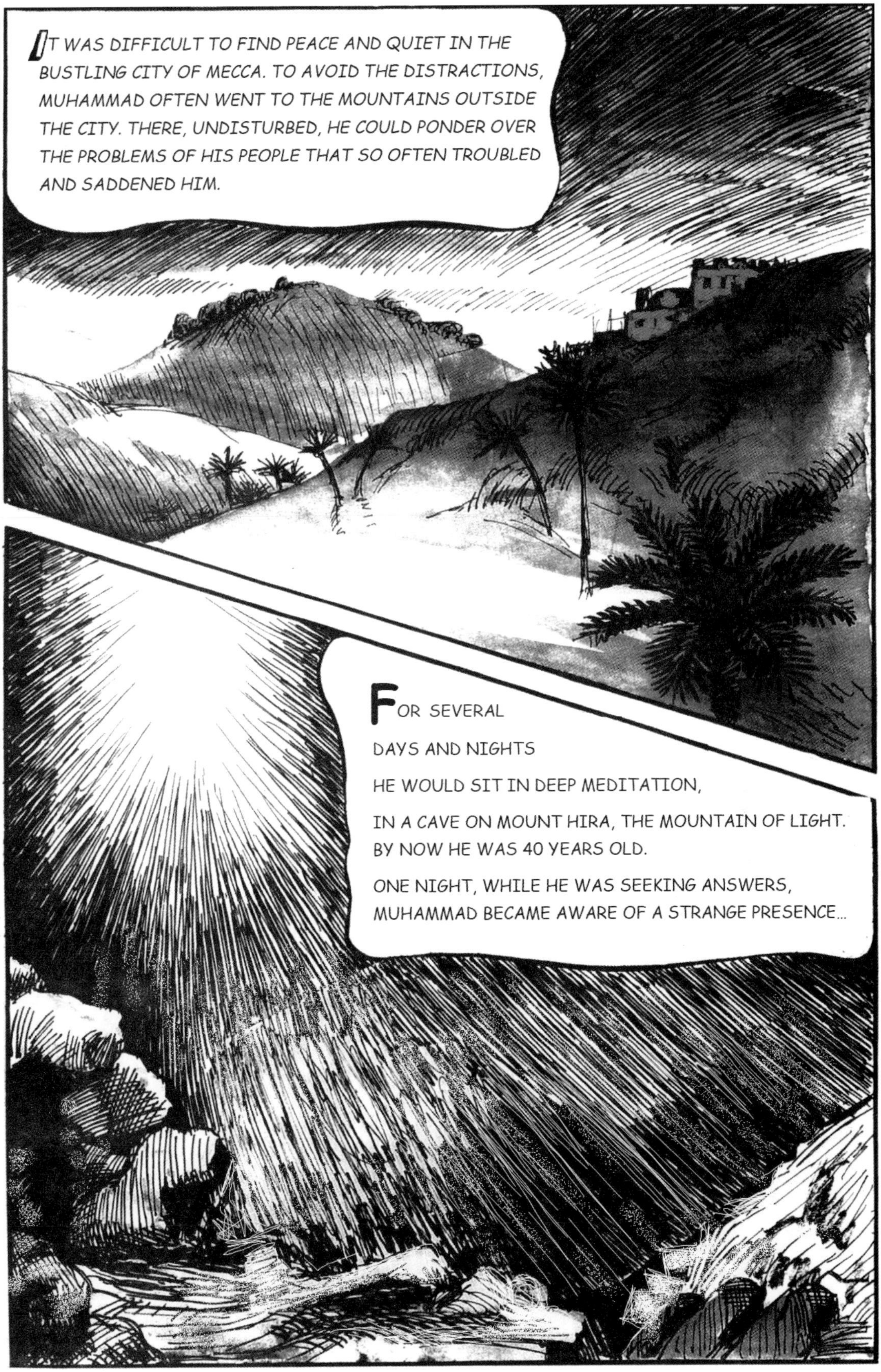
IT WAS DIFFICULT TO FIND PEACE AND QUIET IN THE BUSTLING CITY OF MECCA. TO AVOID THE DISTRACTIONS, MUHAMMAD OFTEN WENT TO THE MOUNTAINS OUTSIDE THE CITY. THERE, UNDISTURBED, HE COULD PONDER OVER THE PROBLEMS OF HIS PEOPLE THAT SO OFTEN TROUBLED AND SADDENED HIM.
FOR SEVERAL DAYS AND NIGHTS HE WOULD SIT IN DEEP MEDITATION, IN A CAVE ON MOUNT HIRA, THE MOUNTAIN OF LIGHT. BY NOW HE WAS 40 YEARS OLD.
ONE NIGHT, WHILE HE WAS SEEKING ANSWERS, MUHAMMAD BECAME AWARE OF A STRANGE PRESENCE...

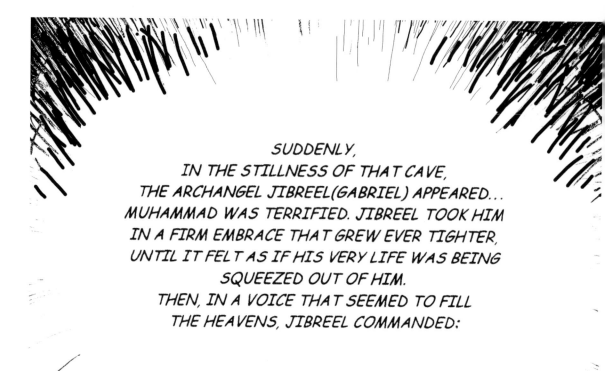

SUDDENLY,
IN THE STILLNESS OF THAT CAVE,
THE ARCHANGEL JIBREEL(GABRIEL) APPEARED...
MUHAMMAD WAS TERRIFIED. JIBREEL TOOK HIM
IN A FIRM EMBRACE THAT GREW EVER TIGHTER,
UNTIL IT FELT AS IF HIS VERY LIFE WAS BEING
SQUEEZED OUT OF HIM.
THEN, IN A VOICE THAT SEEMED TO FILL
THE HEAVENS, JIBREEL COMMANDED:

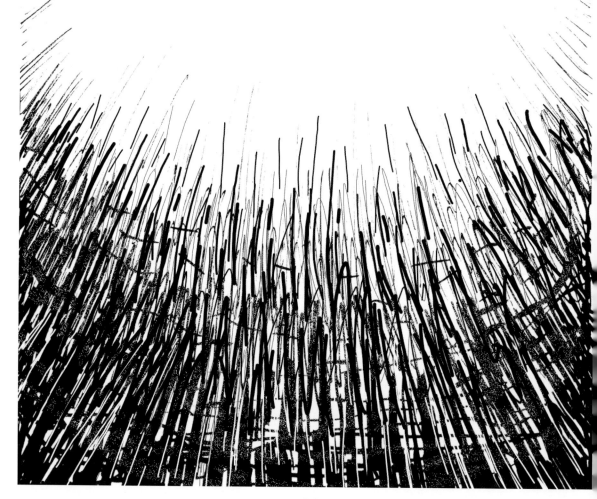

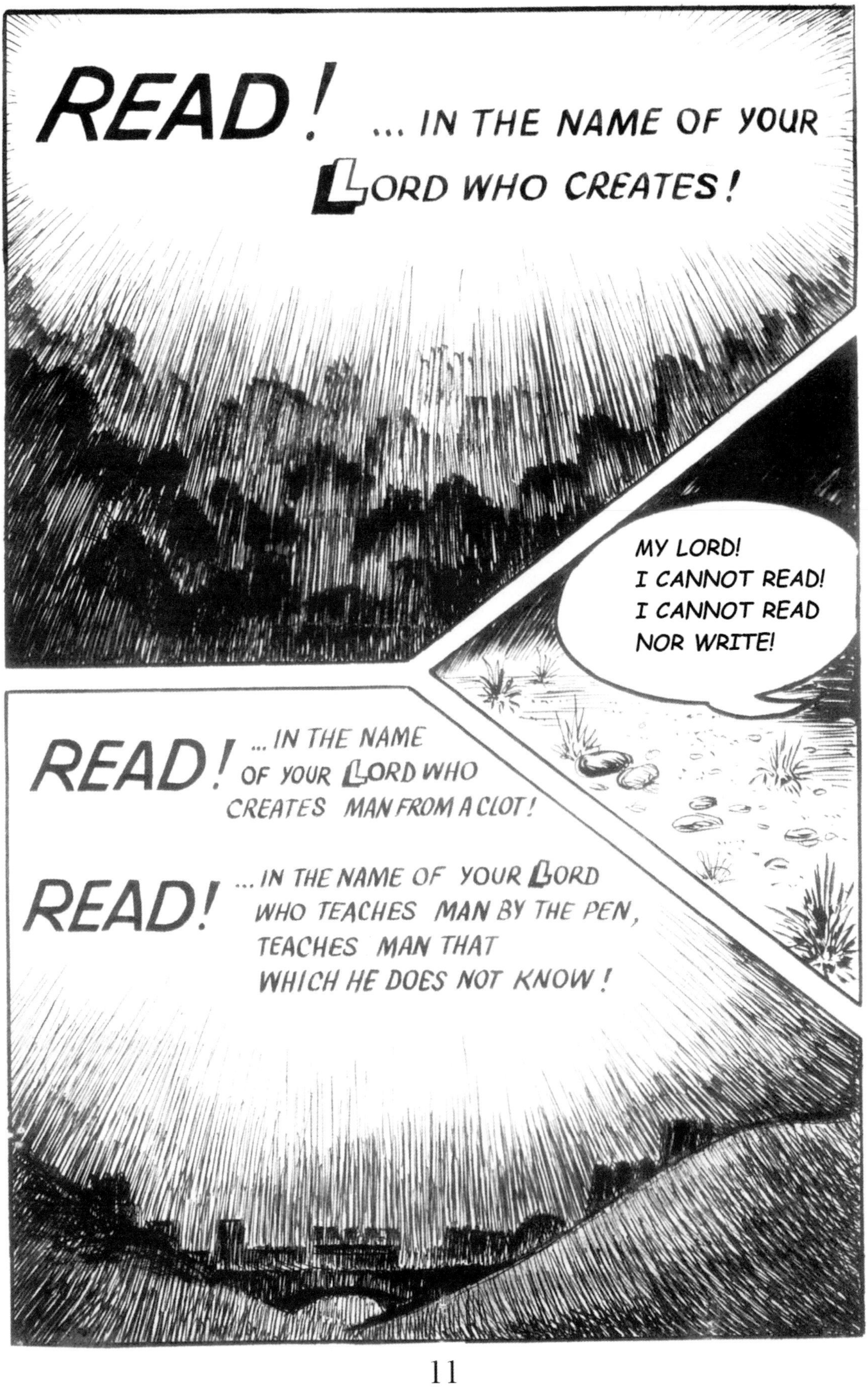
READ! ... IN THE NAME OF YOUR LORD WHO CREATES!
MY LORD! I CANNOT READ! I CANNOT READ NOR WRITE!
READ! ... IN THE NAME OF YOUR LORD WHO CREATES MAN FROM A CLOT!
READ! ... IN THE NAME OF YOUR LORD WHO TEACHES MAN BY THE PEN, TEACHES MAN THAT WHICH HE DOES NOT KNOW!

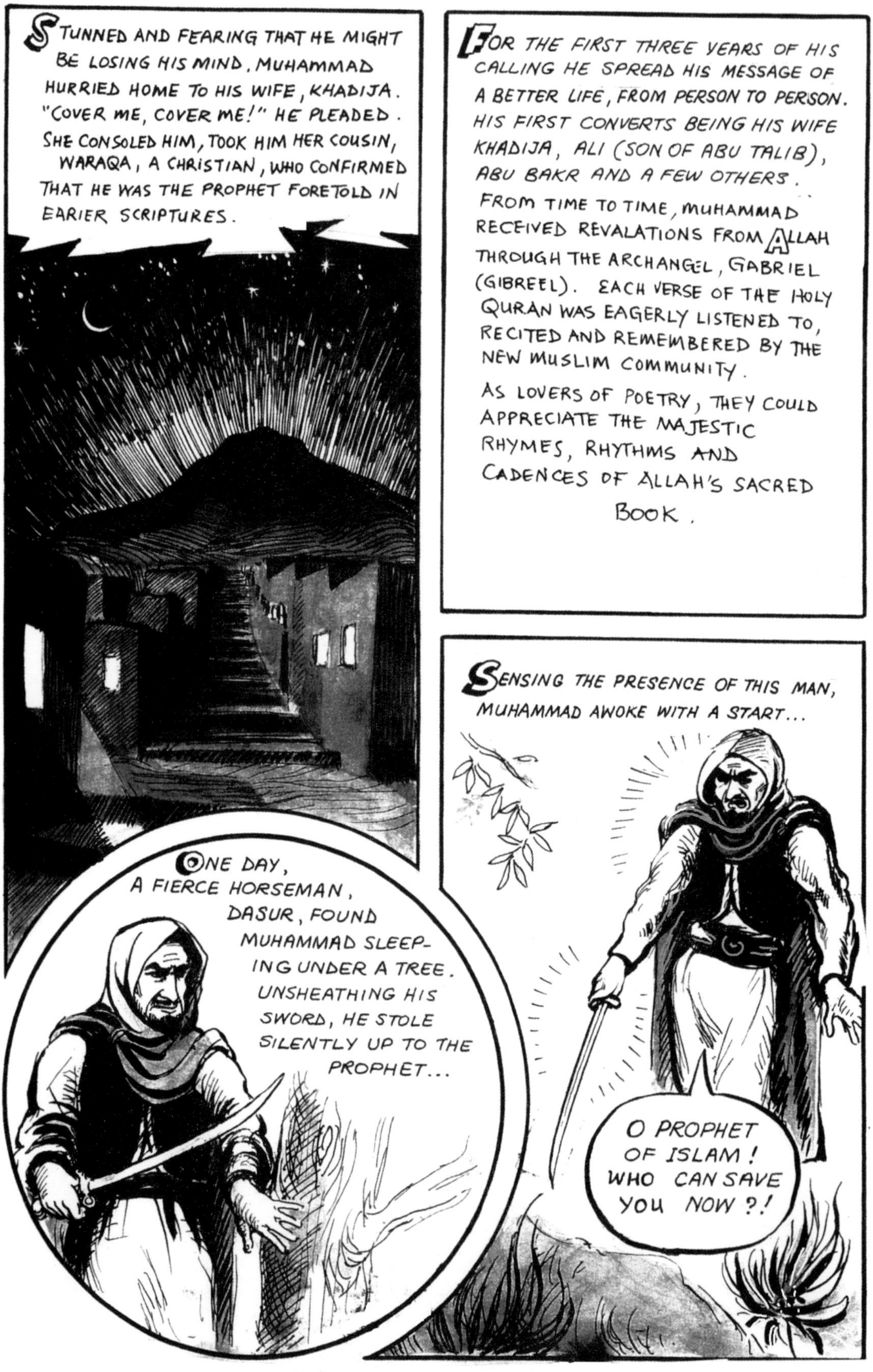
STUNNED AND FEARING THAT HE MIGHT BE LOSING HIS MIND, MUHAMMAD HURRIED HOME TO HIS WIFE, KHADIJA. "COVER ME, COVER ME!" HE PLEADED. SHE CONSOLED HIM, TOOK HIM HER COUSIN, WARAQA, A CHRISTIAN, WHO CONFIRMED THAT HE WAS THE PROPHET FORETOLD IN EARIER SCRIPTURES.
FOR THE FIRST THREE YEARS OF HIS CALLING HE SPREAD HIS MESSAGE OF A BETTER LIFE, FROM PERSON TO PERSON. HIS FIRST CONVERTS BEING HIS WIFE KHADIJA, ALI (SON OF ABU TALIB), ABU BAKR AND A FEW OTHERS.
FROM TIME TO TIME, MUHAMMAD RECEIVED REVALATIONS FROM ALLAH THROUGH THE ARCHANGEL, GABRIEL (GIBREEL). EACH VERSE OF THE HOLY QURAN WAS EAGERLY LISTENED TO, RECITED AND REMEMBERED BY THE NEW MUSLIM COMMUNITY.
AS LOVERS OF POETRY, THEY COULD APPRECIATE THE MAJESTIC RHYMES, RHYTHMS AND CADENCES OF ALLAH'S SACRED BOOK.
ONE DAY, A FIERCE HORSEMAN, DASUR, FOUND MUHAMMAD SLEEPING UNDER A TREE. UNSHEATHING HIS SWORD, HE STOLE SILENTLY UP TO THE PROPHET...
SENSING THE PRESENCE OF THIS MAN, MUHAMMAD AWOKE WITH A START...
O PROPHET OF ISLAM! WHO CAN SAVE YOU NOW?!

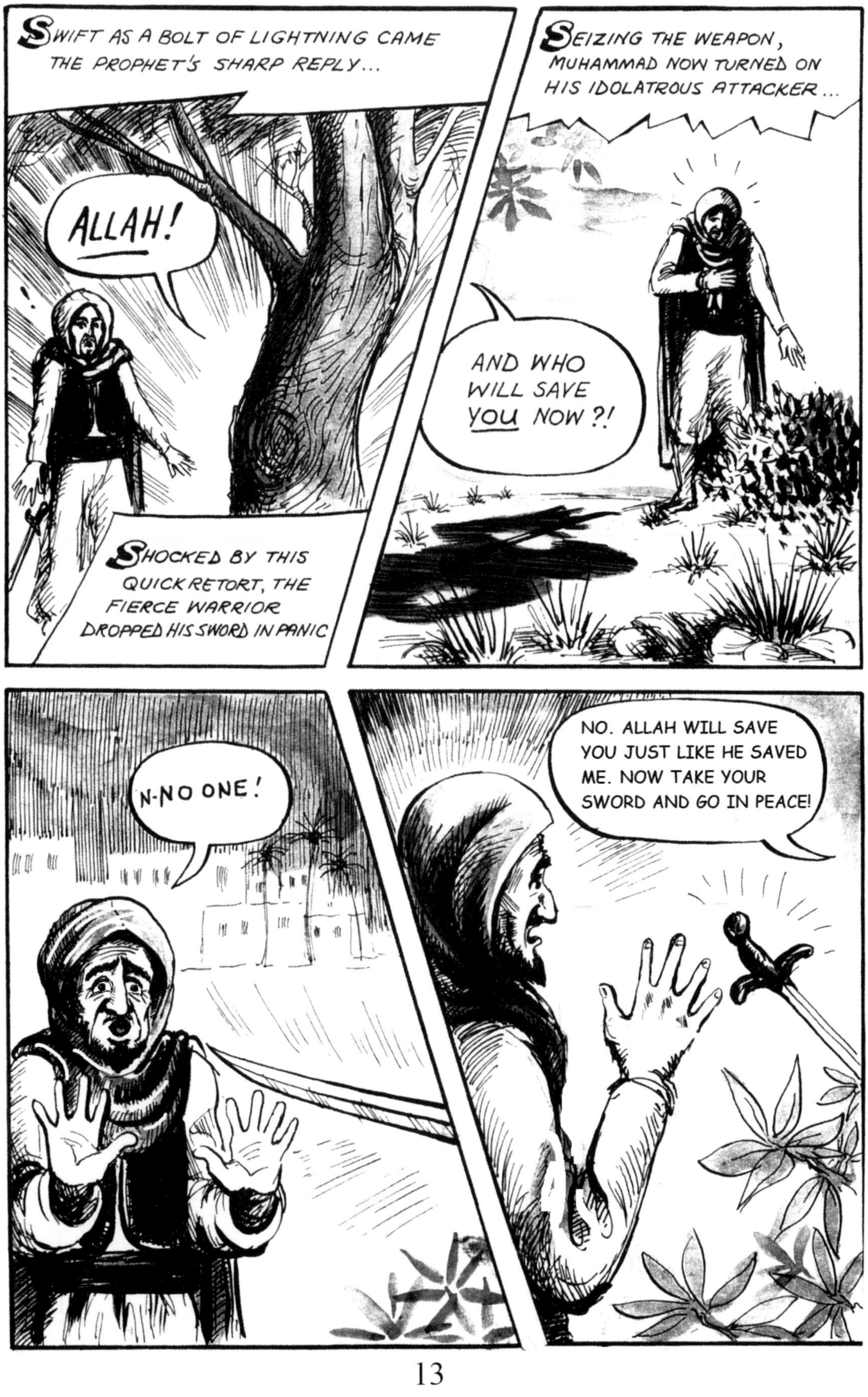
SWIFT AS A BOLT OF LIGHTNING CAME THE PROPHET'S SHARP REPLY...
ALLAH!
SHOCKED BY THIS QUICK RETORT, THE FIERCE WARRIOR DROPPED HIS SWORD IN PANIC
SEIZING THE WEAPON, MUHAMMAD NOW TURNED ON HIS IDOLATROUS ATTACKER...
AND WHO WILL SAVE YOU NOW ?!
N-NO ONE!
NO. ALLAH WILL SAVE YOU JUST LIKE HE SAVED ME. NOW TAKE YOUR SWORD AND GO IN PEACE!

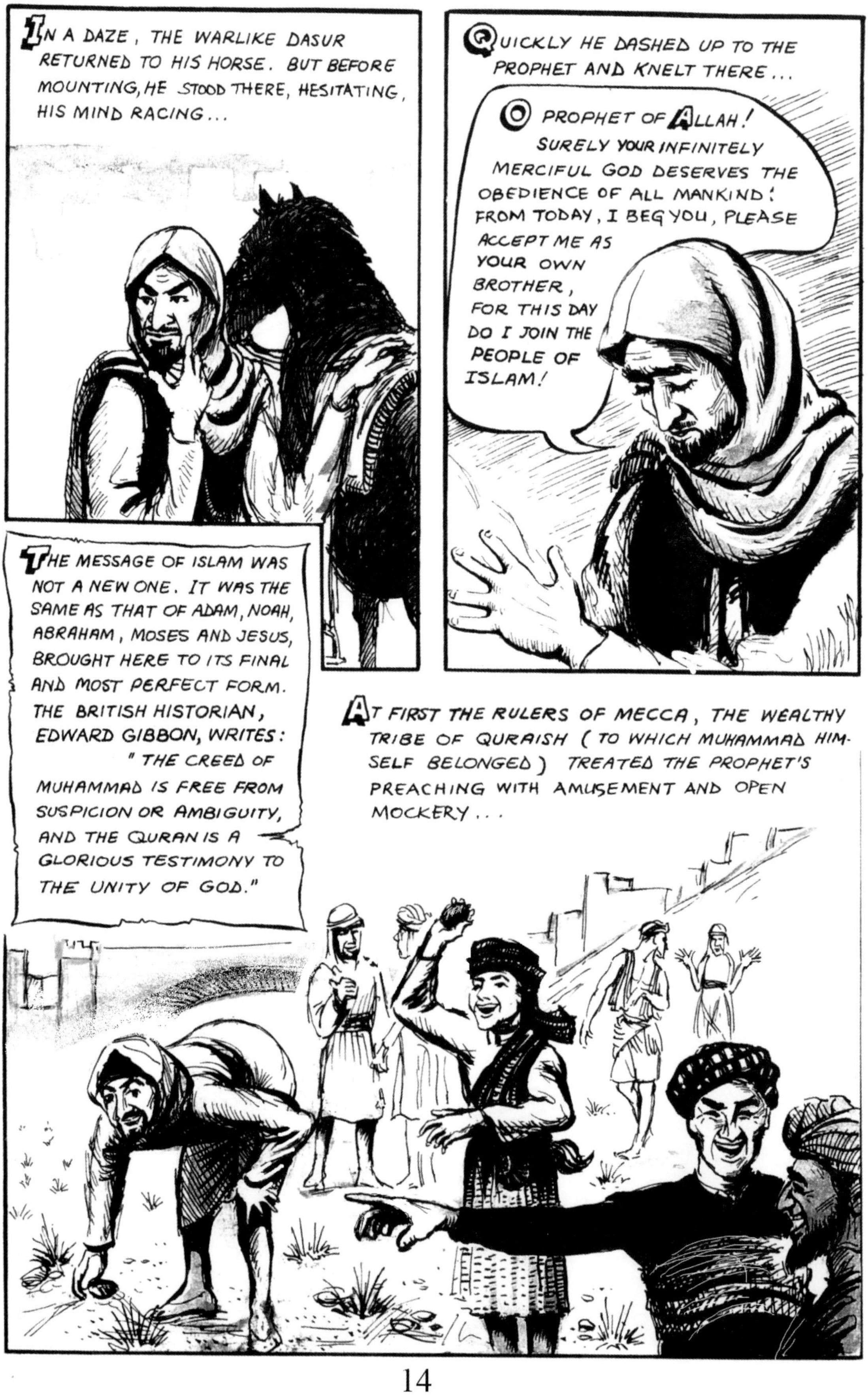
IN A DAZE, THE WARLIKE DASUR RETURNED TO HIS HORSE. BUT BEFORE MOUNTING, HE STOOD THERE, HESITATING, HIS MIND RACING...
QUICKLY HE DASHED UP TO THE PROPHET AND KNELT THERE...
O PROPHET OF ALLAH! SURELY YOUR INFINITELY MERCIFUL GOD DESERVES THE OBEDIENCE OF ALL MANKIND! FROM TODAY, I BEG YOU, PLEASE ACCEPT ME AS YOUR OWN BROTHER, FOR THIS DAY DO I JOIN THE PEOPLE OF ISLAM!
THE MESSAGE OF ISLAM WAS NOT A NEW ONE. IT WAS THE SAME AS THAT OF ADAM, NOAH, ABRAHAM, MOSES AND JESUS, BROUGHT HERE TO ITS FINAL AND MOST PERFECT FORM. THE BRITISH HISTORIAN, EDWARD GIBBON, WRITES: "THE CREED OF MUHAMMAD IS FREE FROM SUSPICION OR AMBIGUITY, AND THE QURAN IS A GLORIOUS TESTIMONY TO THE UNITY OF GOD."
AT FIRST THE RULERS OF MECCA, THE WEALTHY TRIBE OF QURAISH (TO WHICH MUHAMMAD HIMSELF BELONGED) TREATED THE PROPHET'S PREACHING WITH AMUSEMENT AND OPEN MOCKERY...

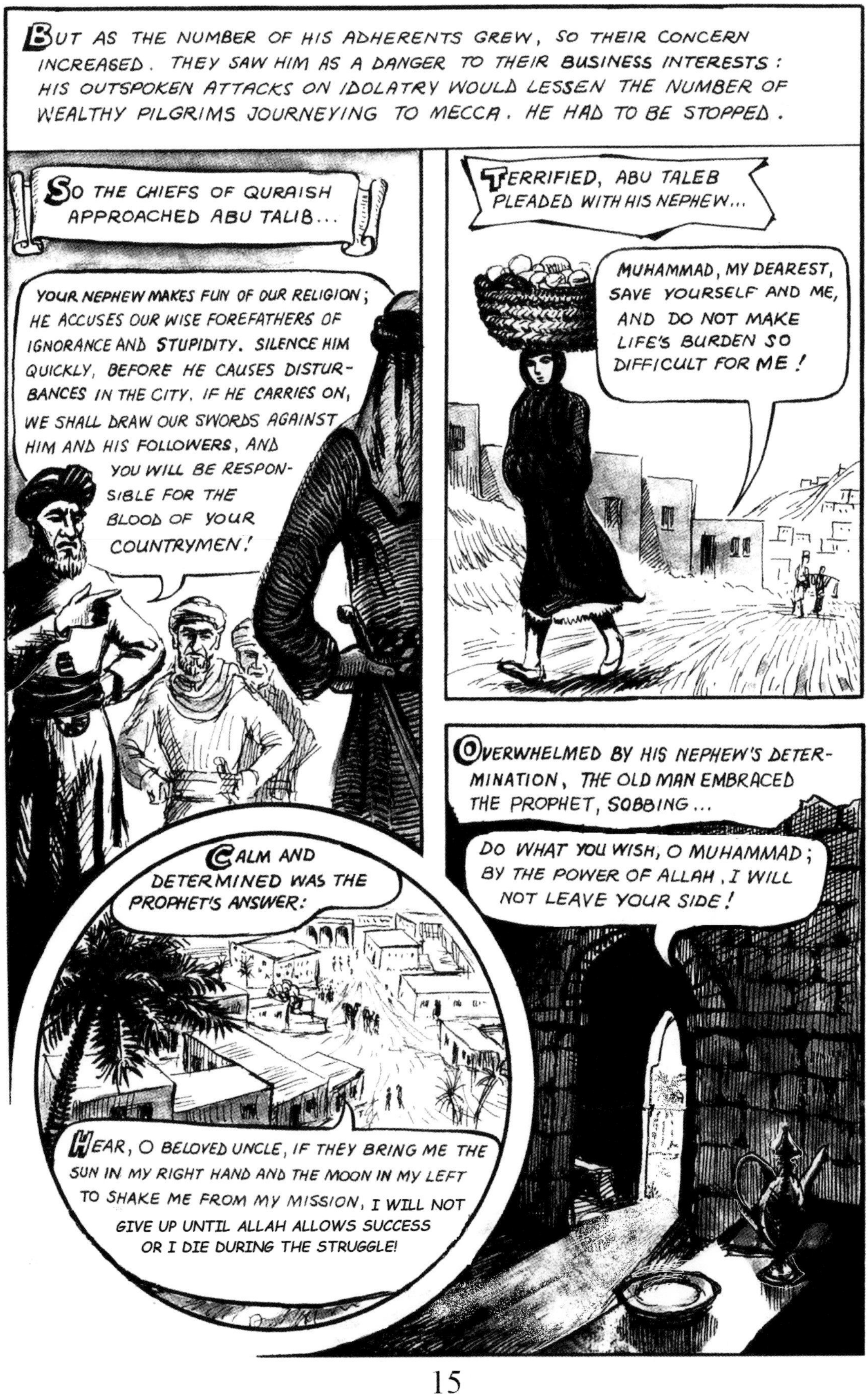

BUT AS THE NUMBER OF HIS ADHERENTS GREW, SO THEIR CONCERN INCREASED. THEY SAW HIM AS A DANGER TO THEIR BUSINESS INTERESTS: HIS OUTSPOKEN ATTACKS ON IDOLATRY WOULD LESSEN THE NUMBER OF WEALTHY PILGRIMS JOURNEYING TO MECCA. HE HAD TO BE STOPPED.
SO THE CHIEFS OF QURAISH APPROACHED ABU TALIB...
YOUR NEPHEW MAKES FUN OF OUR RELIGION; HE ACCUSES OUR WISE FOREFATHERS OF IGNORANCE AND STUPIDITY. SILENCE HIM QUICKLY, BEFORE HE CAUSES DISTURBANCES IN THE CITY. IF HE CARRIES ON, WE SHALL DRAW OUR SWORDS AGAINST HIM AND HIS FOLLOWERS, AND YOU WILL BE RESPONSIBLE FOR THE BLOOD OF YOUR COUNTRYMEN!
TERRIFIED, ABU TALEB PLEADED WITH HIS NEPHEW...
MUHAMMAD, MY DEAREST, SAVE YOURSELF AND ME, AND DO NOT MAKE LIFE'S BURDEN SO DIFFICULT FOR ME!
CALM AND DETERMINED WAS THE PROPHET'S ANSWER:
HEAR, O BELOVED UNCLE, IF THEY BRING ME THE SUN IN MY RIGHT HAND AND THE MOON IN MY LEFT TO SHAKE ME FROM MY MISSION, I WILL NOT GIVE UP UNTIL ALLAH ALLOWS SUCCESS OR I DIE DURING THE STRUGGLE!
OVERWHELMED BY HIS NEPHEW'S DETERMINATION, THE OLD MAN EMBRACED THE PROPHET, SOBBING...
DO WHAT YOU WISH, O MUHAMMAD; BY THE POWER OF ALLAH, I WILL NOT LEAVE YOUR SIDE!

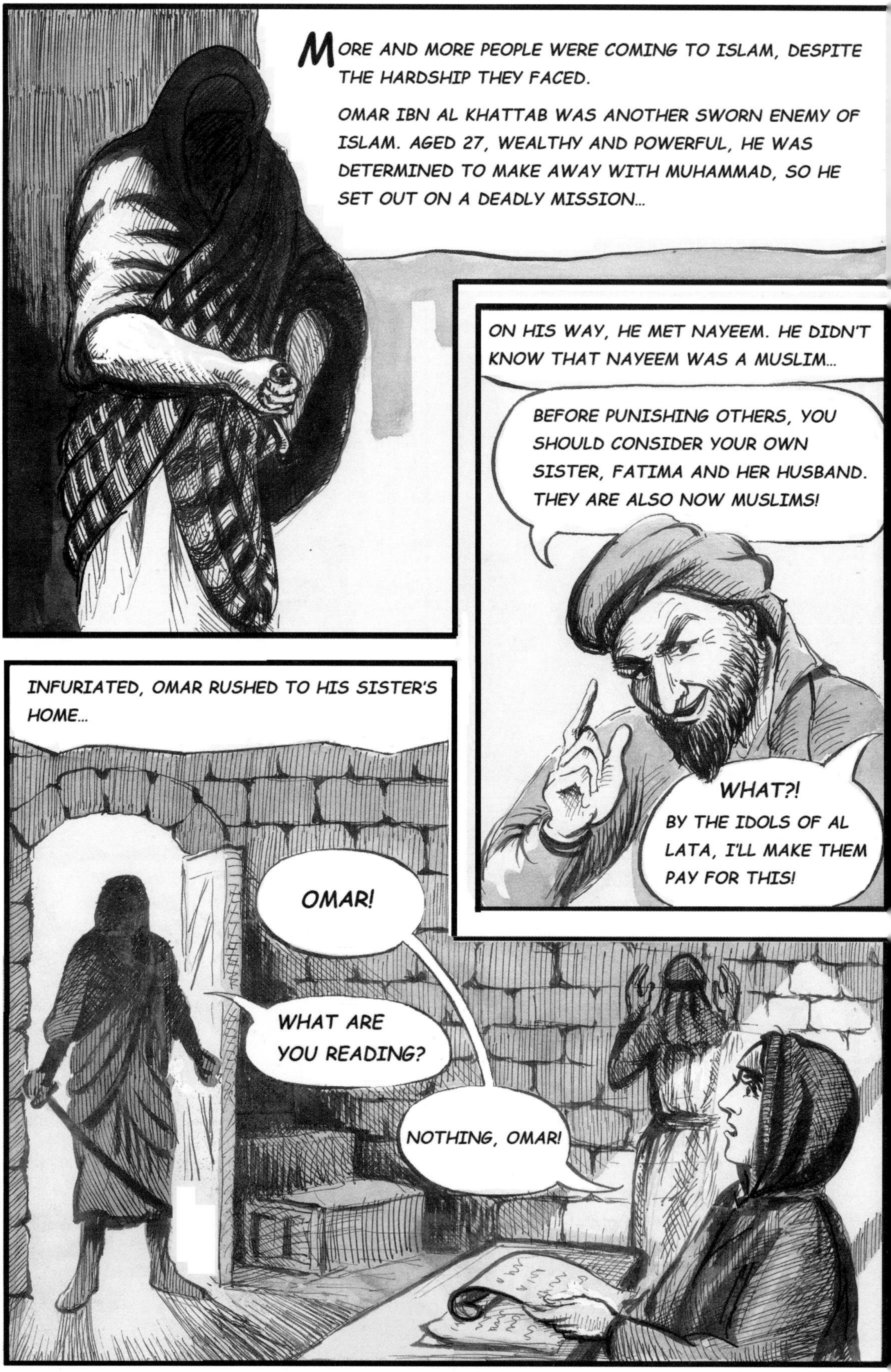
MORE AND MORE PEOPLE WERE COMING TO ISLAM, DESPITE THE HARDSHIP THEY FACED.
OMAR IBN AL KHATTAB WAS ANOTHER SWORN ENEMY OF ISLAM. AGED 27, WEALTHY AND POWERFUL, HE WAS DETERMINED TO MAKE AWAY WITH MUHAMMAD, SO HE SET OUT ON A DEADLY MISSION...
ON HIS WAY, HE MET NAYEEM. HE DIDN'T KNOW THAT NAYEEM WAS A MUSLIM...
BEFORE PUNISHING OTHERS, YOU SHOULD CONSIDER YOUR OWN SISTER, FATIMA AND HER HUSBAND. THEY ARE ALSO NOW MUSLIMS!
WHAT?! BY THE IDOLS OF AL LATA, I'LL MAKE THEM PAY FOR THIS!
INFURIATED, OMAR RUSHED TO HIS SISTER'S HOME...
OMAR!
WHAT ARE YOU READING?
NOTHING, OMAR!

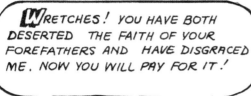
WRETCHES! YOU HAVE BOTH DESERTED THE FAITH OF YOUR FOREFATHERS AND HAVE DISGRACED ME. NOW YOU WILL PAY FOR IT!

NO, OMAR! LEAVE HIM ALONE!

AFTER ATTACKING SAYEED, OMAR TURNED TO HIS SISTER AND BEAT HER TILL THE BLOOD FLOWED...

NOW, WHAT HAVE YOU TO SAY FOR YOURSELVES?

O, OMAR! I AM A **MUSLIM**, AND I SHALL REMAIN SO EVEN IF I HAVE TO BE MURDERED FOR IT!

TOUCHED BY THE STRENGTH OF HER FAITH, HE AGAIN ASKED HER ABOUT THE BOOK SHE WAS READING. SHE HANDED HIM THE STRANGE PARCHMENT SHEETS ON WHICH MANY VERSES WERE WRITTEN...

"WE HAVE NOT SENT DOWN THIS QUR'AN TO CAUSE YOU ANY DISTRESS, BUT ONLY AS A REMINDER TO THOSE WHO FEAR ALLAH (MOST HIGH)

AS OMAR READ THE OPENING VERSES OF SURA TA-HA, A CHANGE CAME OVER HIM. HIS VOICE LOWERED, HIS ANGER SOFTENED, HIS HEART MELTED. ALLAH CAME BETWEEN OMAR AND HIS HEART...

"THE ALL-MERCIFUL, ESTABLISHED ON THE THRONE OF AUTHORITY. TO HIM BELONGS WHATEVER IS IN THE HEAVENS, OR ON EARTH, OR BENEATH THE SOIL...

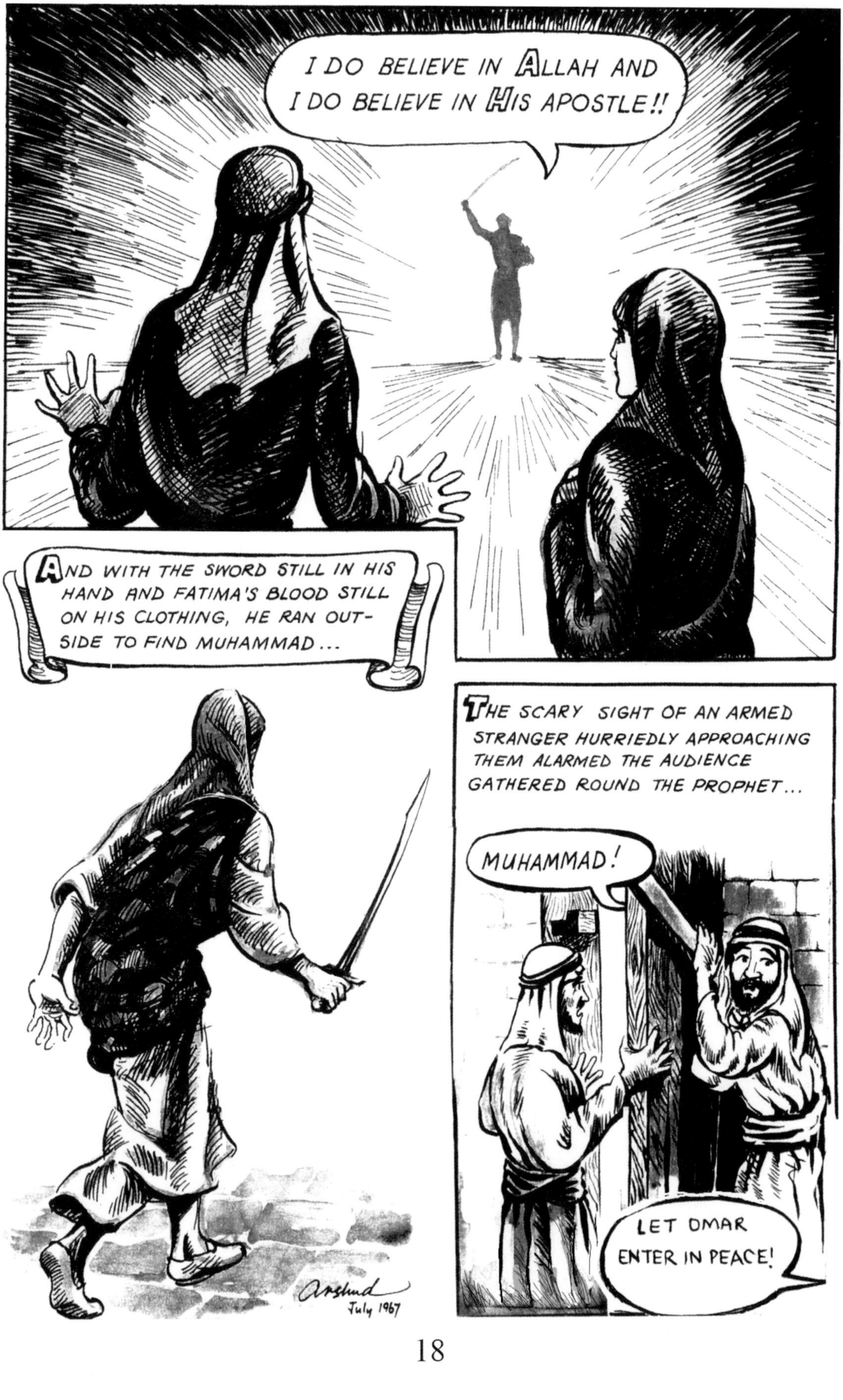
I DO BELIEVE IN ALLAH AND I DO BELIEVE IN HIS APOSTLE!!
AND WITH THE SWORD STILL IN HIS HAND AND FATIMA'S BLOOD STILL ON HIS CLOTHING, HE RAN OUTSIDE TO FIND MUHAMMAD...
THE SCARY SIGHT OF AN ARMED STRANGER HURRIEDLY APPROACHING THEM ALARMED THE AUDIENCE GATHERED ROUND THE PROPHET...
MUHAMMAD!
LET OMAR ENTER IN PEACE!
Arshad
July 1967

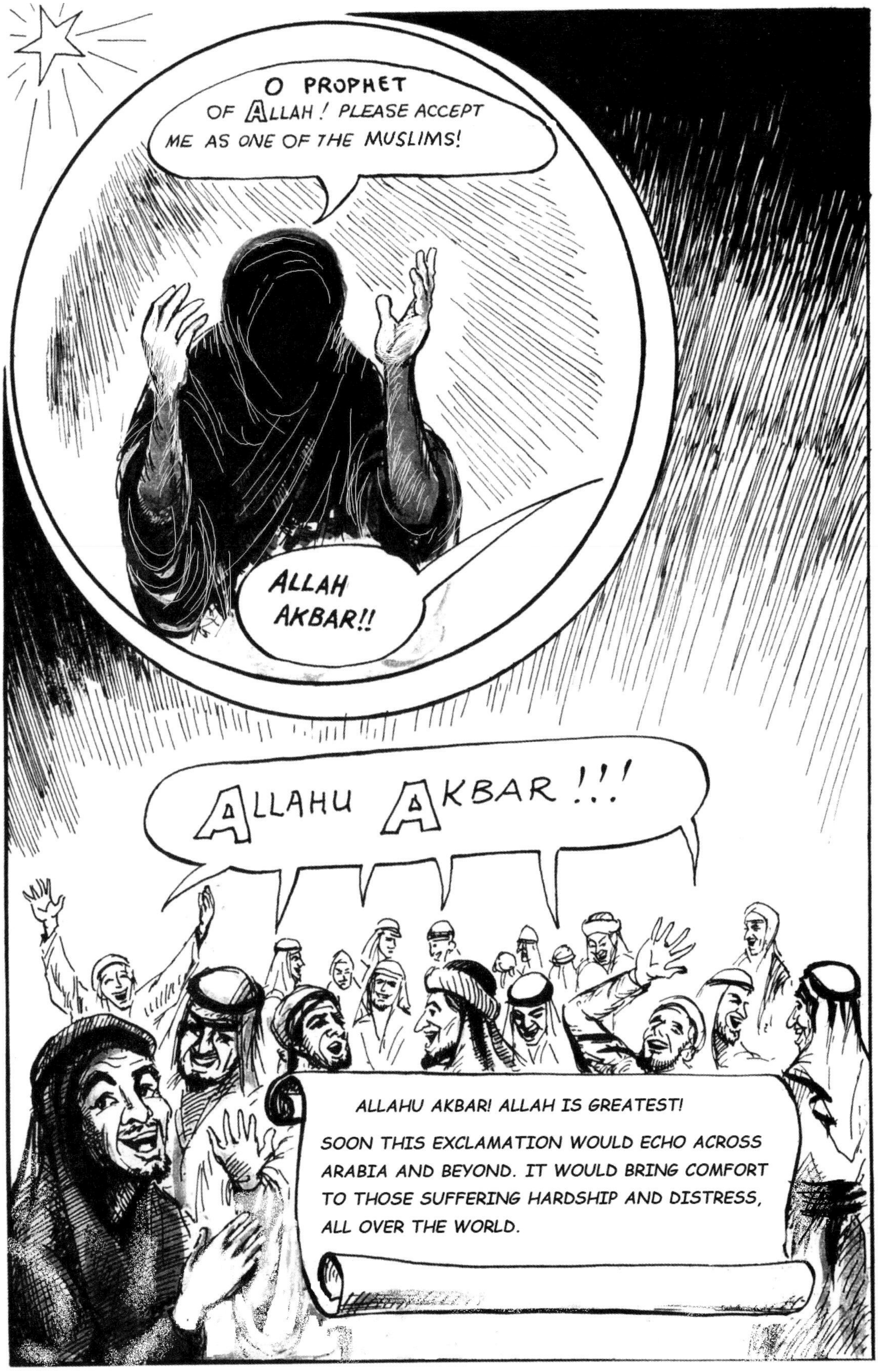
O PROPHET OF ALLAH! PLEASE ACCEPT ME AS ONE OF THE MUSLIMS!
ALLAH AKBAR!!
ALLAHU AKBAR!!!
ALLAHU AKBAR! ALLAH IS GREATEST!
SOON THIS EXCLAMATION WOULD ECHO ACROSS ARABIA AND BEYOND. IT WOULD BRING COMFORT TO THOSE SUFFERING HARDSHIP AND DISTRESS, ALL OVER THE WORLD.

CHAPTER THREE:

Hijra

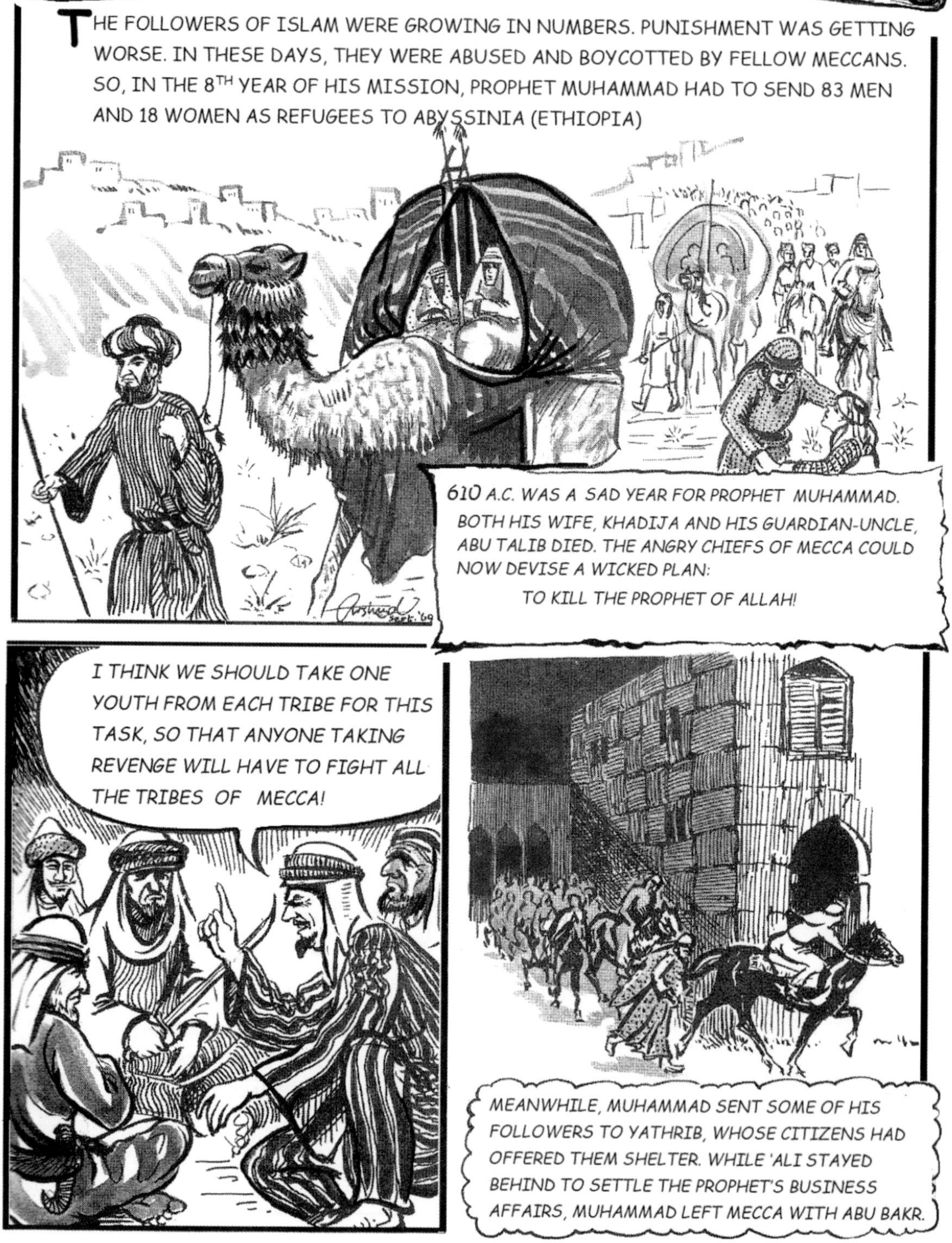
THE FOLLOWERS OF ISLAM WERE GROWING IN NUMBERS. PUNISHMENT WAS GETTING WORSE. IN THESE DAYS, THEY WERE ABUSED AND BOYCOTTED BY FELLOW MECCANS. SO, IN THE 8TH YEAR OF HIS MISSION, PROPHET MUHAMMAD HAD TO SEND 83 MEN AND 18 WOMEN AS REFUGEES TO ABYSSINIA (ETHIOPIA)
610 A.C. WAS A SAD YEAR FOR PROPHET MUHAMMAD. BOTH HIS WIFE, KHADIJA AND HIS GUARDIAN-UNCLE, ABU TALIB DIED. THE ANGRY CHIEFS OF MECCA COULD NOW DEVISE A WICKED PLAN: TO KILL THE PROPHET OF ALLAH!
I THINK WE SHOULD TAKE ONE YOUTH FROM EACH TRIBE FOR THIS TASK, SO THAT ANYONE TAKING REVENGE WILL HAVE TO FIGHT ALL THE TRIBES OF MECCA!
MEANWHILE, MUHAMMAD SENT SOME OF HIS FOLLOWERS TO YATHRIB, WHOSE CITIZENS HAD OFFERED THEM SHELTER. WHILE 'ALI STAYED BEHIND TO SETTLE THE PROPHET'S BUSINESS AFFAIRS, MUHAMMAD LEFT MECCA WITH ABU BAKR.

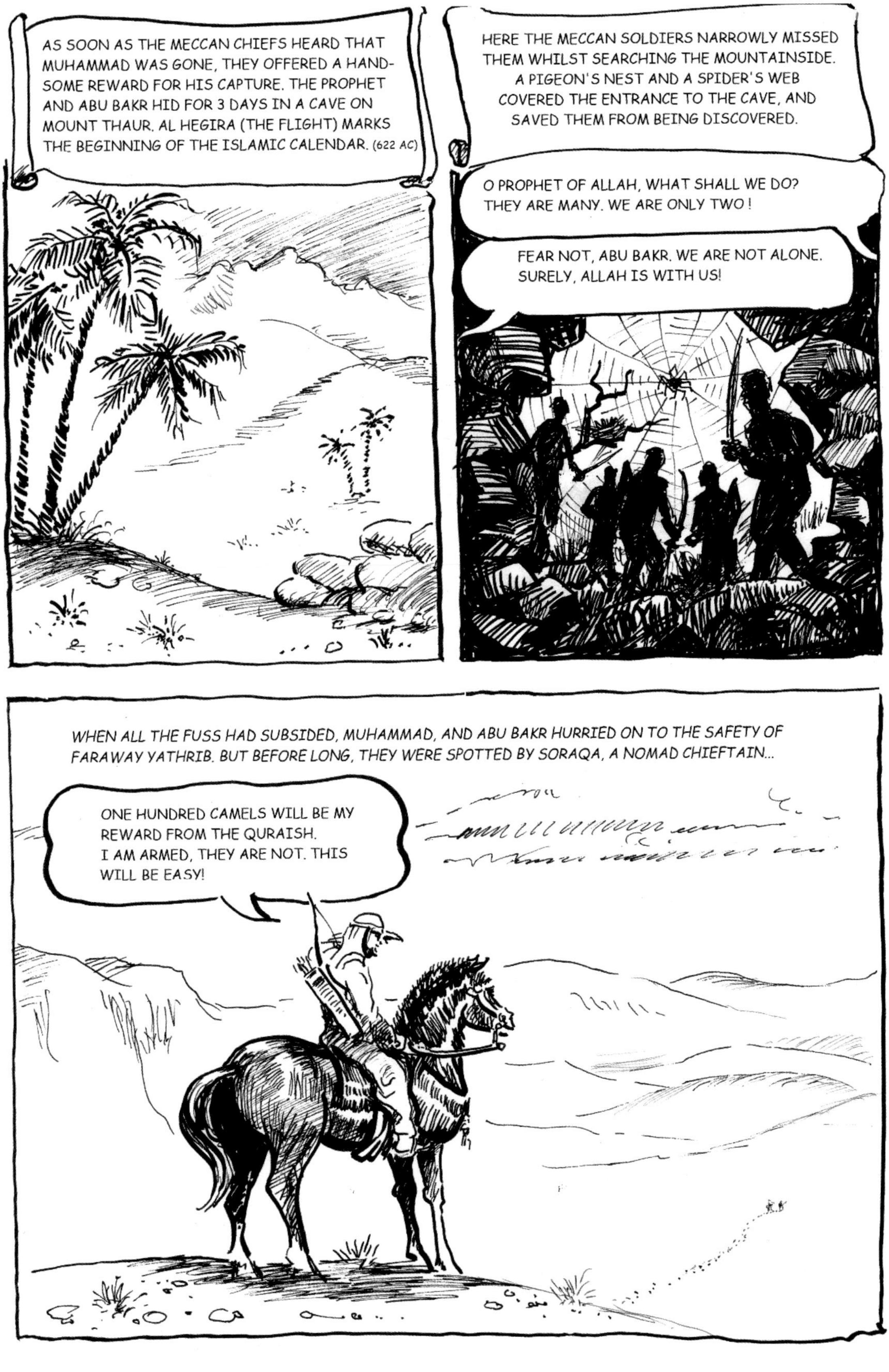
AS SOON AS THE MECCAN CHIEFS HEARD THAT MUHAMMAD WAS GONE, THEY OFFERED A HANDSOME REWARD FOR HIS CAPTURE. THE PROPHET AND ABU BAKR HID FOR 3 DAYS IN A CAVE ON MOUNT THAUR. AL HEGIRA (THE FLIGHT) MARKS THE BEGINNING OF THE ISLAMIC CALENDAR. (622 AC)
HERE THE MECCAN SOLDIERS NARROWLY MISSED THEM WHILST SEARCHING THE MOUNTAINSIDE. A PIGEON'S NEST AND A SPIDER'S WEB COVERED THE ENTRANCE TO THE CAVE, AND SAVED THEM FROM BEING DISCOVERED.
O PROPHET OF ALLAH, WHAT SHALL WE DO? THEY ARE MANY. WE ARE ONLY TWO !
FEAR NOT, ABU BAKR. WE ARE NOT ALONE. SURELY, ALLAH IS WITH US!
WHEN ALL THE FUSS HAD SUBSIDED, MUHAMMAD, AND ABU BAKR HURRIED ON TO THE SAFETY OF FARAWAY YATHRIB. BUT BEFORE LONG, THEY WERE SPOTTED BY SORAQA, A NOMAD CHIEFTAIN...
ONE HUNDRED CAMELS WILL BE MY REWARD FROM THE QURAISH. I AM ARMED, THEY ARE NOT. THIS WILL BE EASY!

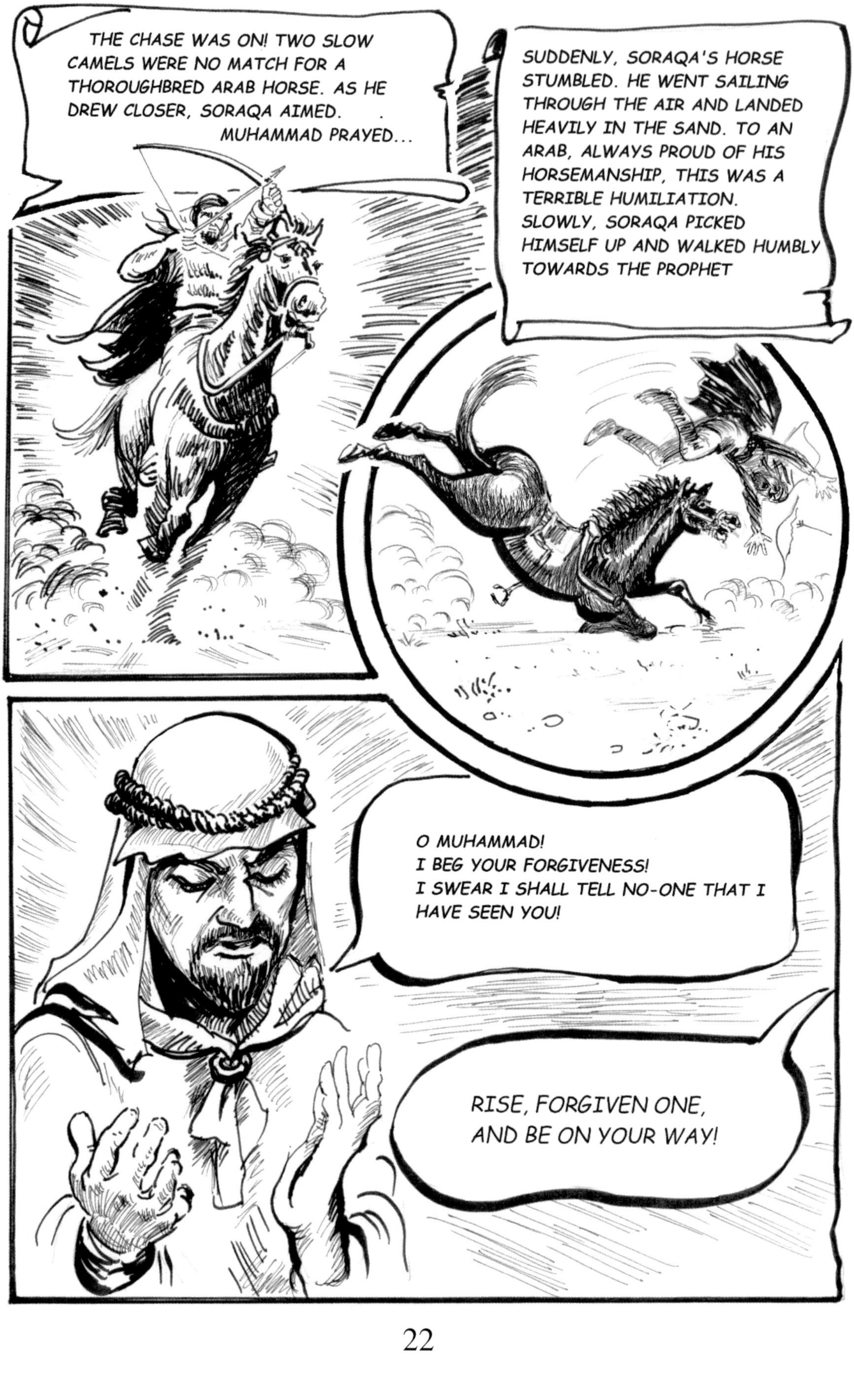
THE CHASE WAS ON! TWO SLOW CAMELS WERE NO MATCH FOR A THOROUGHBRED ARAB HORSE. AS HE DREW CLOSER, SORAQA AIMED. MUHAMMAD PRAYED...
SUDDENLY, SORAQA'S HORSE STUMBLED. HE WENT SAILING THROUGH THE AIR AND LANDED HEAVILY IN THE SAND. TO AN ARAB, ALWAYS PROUD OF HIS HORSEMANSHIP, THIS WAS A TERRIBLE HUMILIATION. SLOWLY, SORAQA PICKED HIMSELF UP AND WALKED HUMBLY TOWARDS THE PROPHET
O MUHAMMAD! I BEG YOUR FORGIVENESS! I SWEAR I SHALL TELL NO-ONE THAT I HAVE SEEN YOU!
RISE, FORGIVEN ONE, AND BE ON YOUR WAY!

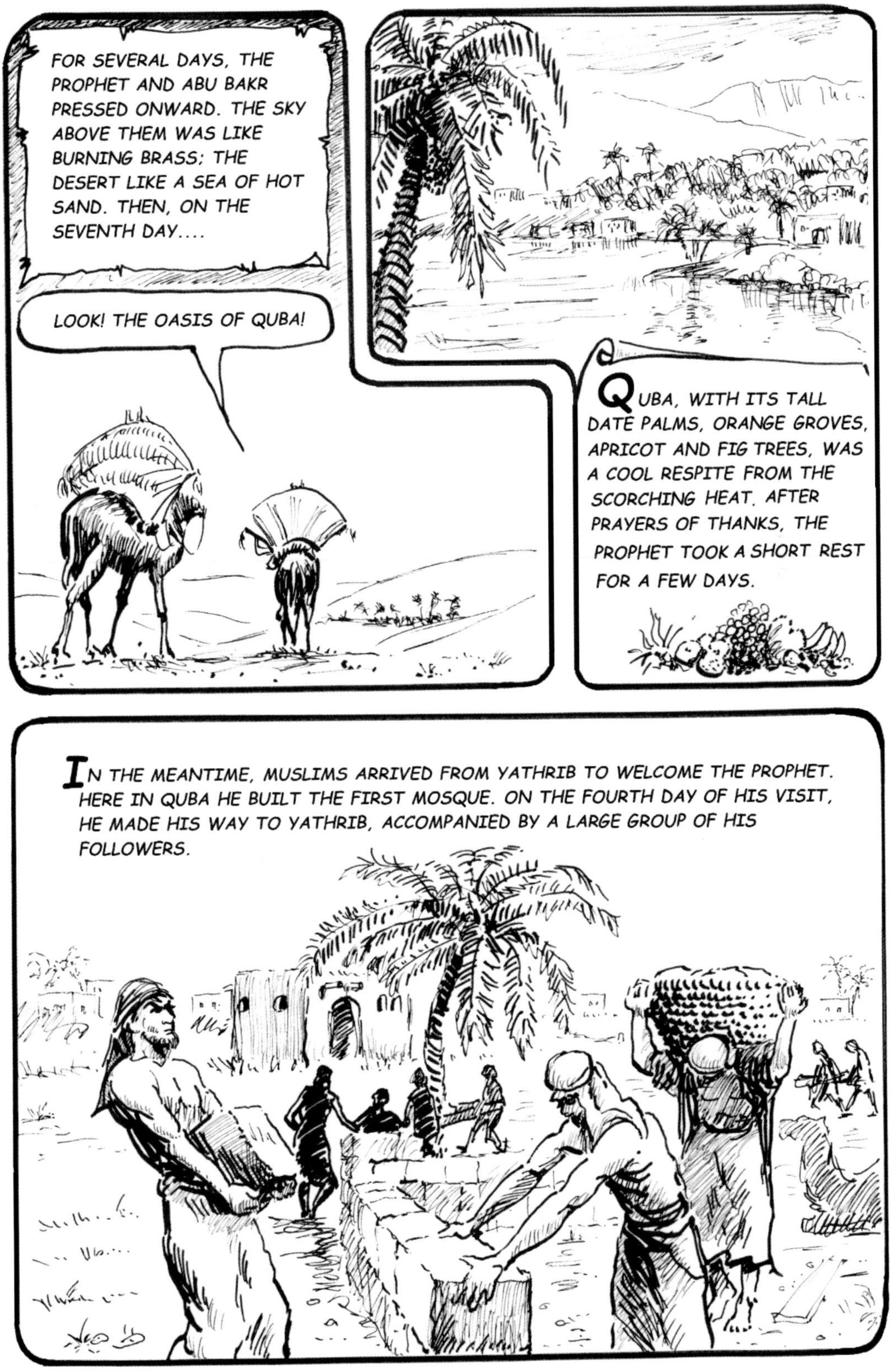
FOR SEVERAL DAYS, THE PROPHET AND ABU BAKR PRESSED ONWARD. THE SKY ABOVE THEM WAS LIKE BURNING BRASS; THE DESERT LIKE A SEA OF HOT SAND. THEN, ON THE SEVENTH DAY....
LOOK! THE OASIS OF QUBA!
QUBA, WITH ITS TALL DATE PALMS, ORANGE GROVES, APRICOT AND FIG TREES, WAS A COOL RESPITE FROM THE SCORCHING HEAT. AFTER PRAYERS OF THANKS, THE PROPHET TOOK A SHORT REST FOR A FEW DAYS.
IN THE MEANTIME, MUSLIMS ARRIVED FROM YATHRIB TO WELCOME THE PROPHET. HERE IN QUBA HE BUILT THE FIRST MOSQUE. ON THE FOURTH DAY OF HIS VISIT, HE MADE HIS WAY TO YATHRIB, ACCOMPANIED BY A LARGE GROUP OF HIS FOLLOWERS.

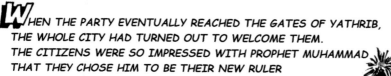

CHAPTER FOUR

Medinat-un-Nabi

WHEN THE PARTY EVENTUALLY REACHED THE GATES OF YATHRIB, THE WHOLE CITY HAD TURNED OUT TO WELCOME THEM. THE CITIZENS WERE SO IMPRESSED WITH PROPHET MUHAMMAD THAT THEY CHOSE HIM TO BE THEIR NEW RULER

MUHAMMAD THE PREACHER NOW BECAME MUHAMMAD THE STATESMAN, RULER OF YATHRIB. THE CITY WAS RENAMED: "MEDINATUN NABI" MEANING "CITY OF THE PROPHET"

AT FIRST, HE BUILT THE BONDS OF BROTHERHOOD BETWEEN THE REFUGEES AND THEIR HELPERS, AND BETWEEN THE WARRING TRIBES OF AUS AND KHASRAJ.

ASSALAAM-ALAIKUM —AND HOW ARE YOU, BROTHER YUSUF?!

THIS WAS SOMETHING NEW TO THE ARABS, WHO USUALLY REGARDED PEOPLE FROM OTHER TRIBES AS RIVALS OR ENEMIES.

THE JEWS OF MEDINA WERE GRANTED FULL CULTURAL AND RELIGIOUS FREEDOM. THEY WERE ONLY REQUIRED TO SUPPORT THE PROPHET IF THE CITY WAS ATTACKED FROM OUTSIDE.

IN MEDINA HE SET UP HISTORY'S FIRST WRITTEN CONSTITUTION WHERE ALL CITIZENS INCLUDING MINORITY GROUPS WERE GUARANTEED EQUAL RIGHTS.

THEN HE PUT SOME SCOUTS OUTSIDE THE CITY. THEY WERE TO WATCH OUT FOR POSSIBLE ATTACKS.

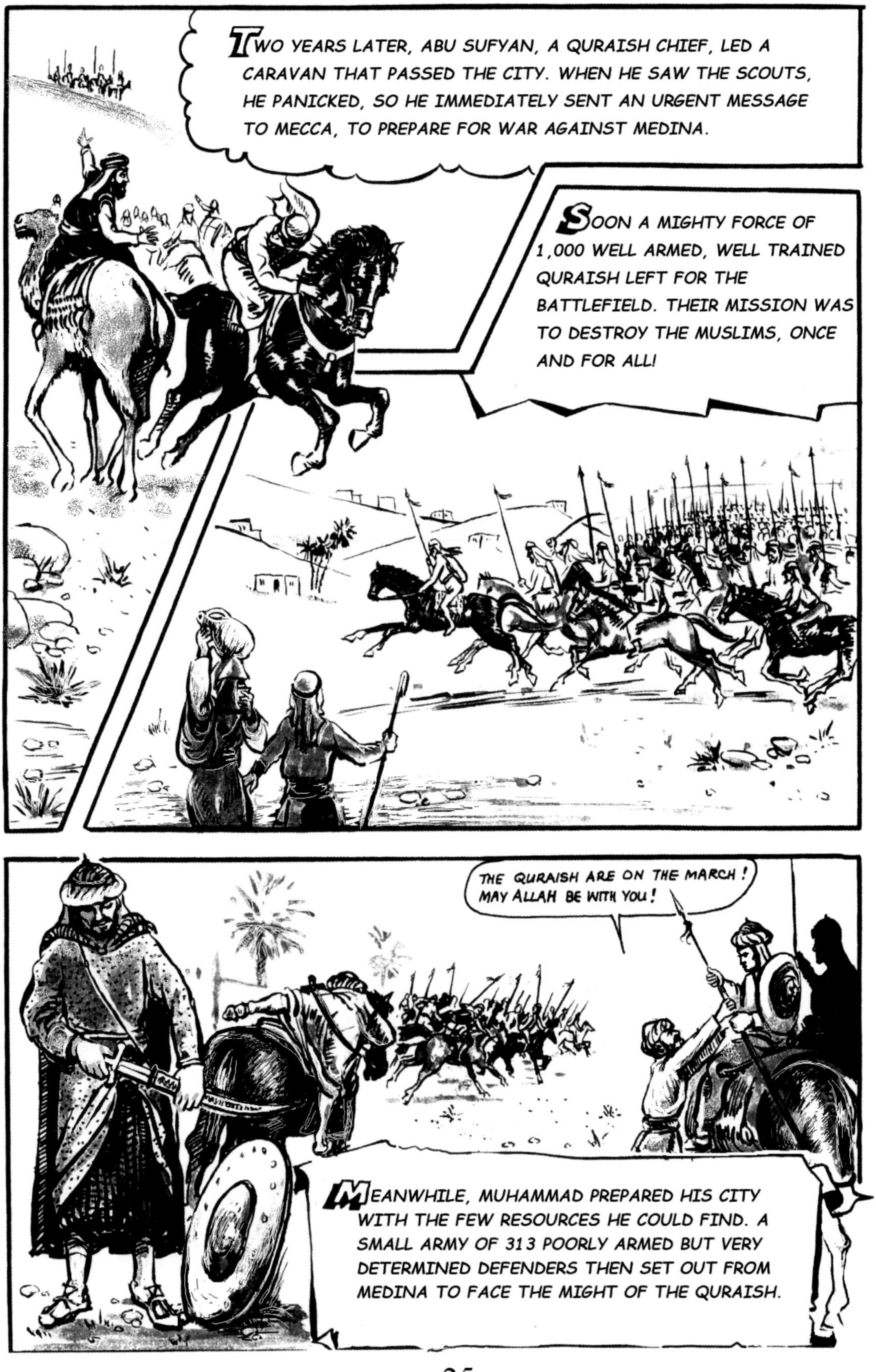
TWO YEARS LATER, ABU SUFYAN, A QURAISH CHIEF, LED A CARAVAN THAT PASSED THE CITY. WHEN HE SAW THE SCOUTS, HE PANICKED, SO HE IMMEDIATELY SENT AN URGENT MESSAGE TO MECCA, TO PREPARE FOR WAR AGAINST MEDINA.
SOON A MIGHTY FORCE OF 1,000 WELL ARMED, WELL TRAINED QURAISH LEFT FOR THE BATTLEFIELD. THEIR MISSION WAS TO DESTROY THE MUSLIMS, ONCE AND FOR ALL!
THE QURAISH ARE ON THE MARCH! MAY ALLAH BE WITH YOU!
MEANWHILE, MUHAMMAD PREPARED HIS CITY WITH THE FEW RESOURCES HE COULD FIND. A SMALL ARMY OF 313 POORLY ARMED BUT VERY DETERMINED DEFENDERS THEN SET OUT FROM MEDINA TO FACE THE MIGHT OF THE QURAISH.

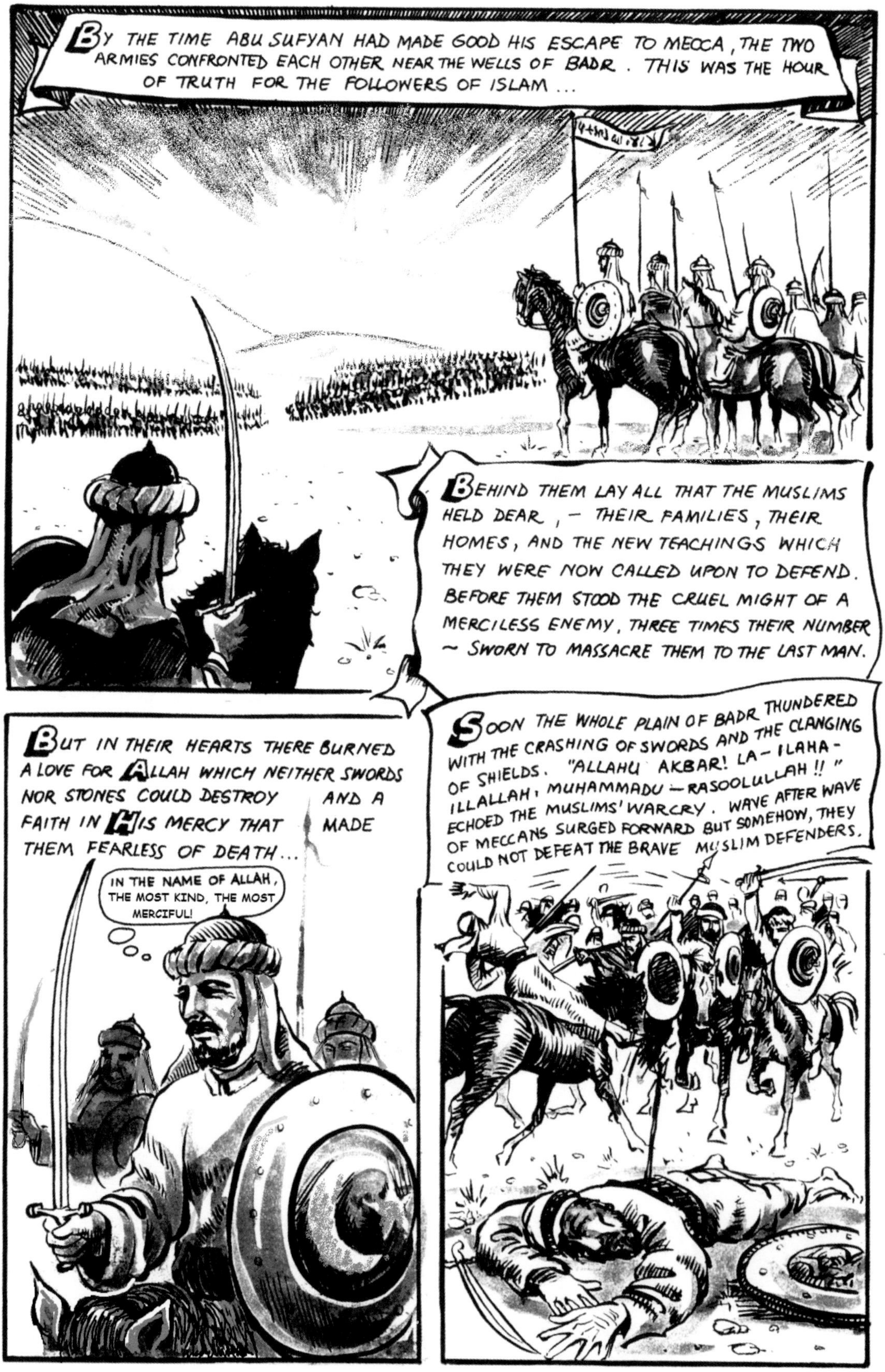
BY THE TIME ABU SUFYAN HAD MADE GOOD HIS ESCAPE TO MECCA, THE TWO ARMIES CONFRONTED EACH OTHER NEAR THE WELLS OF BADR. THIS WAS THE HOUR OF TRUTH FOR THE FOLLOWERS OF ISLAM...
BEHIND THEM LAY ALL THAT THE MUSLIMS HELD DEAR, – THEIR FAMILIES, THEIR HOMES, AND THE NEW TEACHINGS WHICH THEY WERE NOW CALLED UPON TO DEFEND. BEFORE THEM STOOD THE CRUEL MIGHT OF A MERCILESS ENEMY, THREE TIMES THEIR NUMBER ~ SWORN TO MASSACRE THEM TO THE LAST MAN.
BUT IN THEIR HEARTS THERE BURNED A LOVE FOR ALLAH WHICH NEITHER SWORDS NOR STONES COULD DESTROY AND A FAITH IN HIS MERCY THAT MADE THEM FEARLESS OF DEATH...
IN THE NAME OF ALLAH, THE MOST KIND, THE MOST MERCIFUL!
SOON THE WHOLE PLAIN OF BADR THUNDERED WITH THE CRASHING OF SWORDS AND THE CLANGING OF SHIELDS. "ALLAHU AKBAR! LA-ILAHA-ILLALLAH, MUHAMMADU – RASOOLULLAH!!" ECHOED THE MUSLIMS' WARCRY. WAVE AFTER WAVE OF MECCANS SURGED FORWARD BUT SOMEHOW, THEY COULD NOT DEFEAT THE BRAVE MUSLIM DEFENDERS.

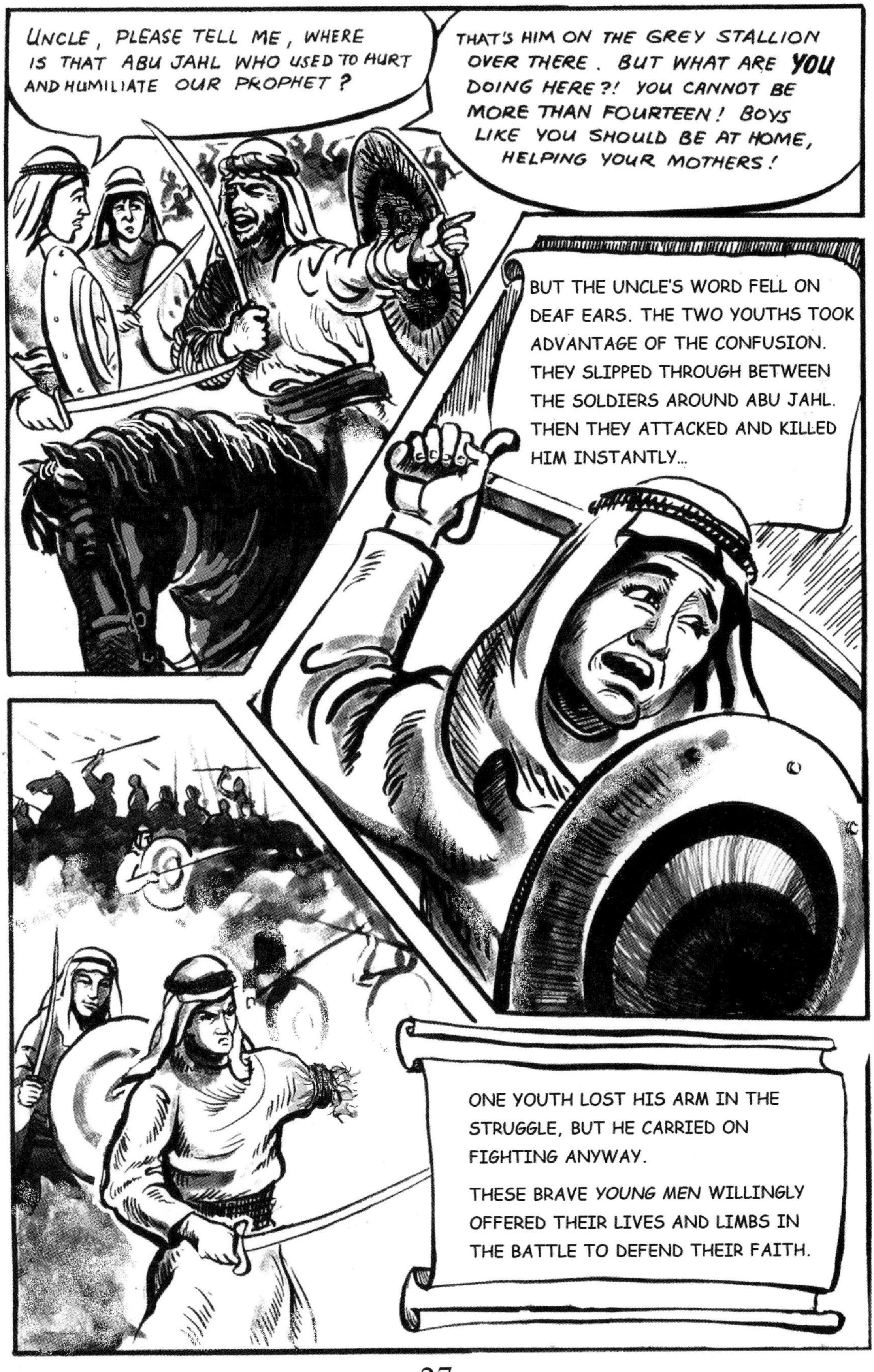

UNCLE, PLEASE TELL ME, WHERE IS THAT ABU JAHL WHO USED TO HURT AND HUMILIATE OUR PROPHET?
THAT'S HIM ON THE GREY STALLION OVER THERE. BUT WHAT ARE YOU DOING HERE?! YOU CANNOT BE MORE THAN FOURTEEN! BOYS LIKE YOU SHOULD BE AT HOME, HELPING YOUR MOTHERS!
BUT THE UNCLE'S WORD FELL ON DEAF EARS. THE TWO YOUTHS TOOK ADVANTAGE OF THE CONFUSION. THEY SLIPPED THROUGH BETWEEN THE SOLDIERS AROUND ABU JAHL. THEN THEY ATTACKED AND KILLED HIM INSTANTLY...
ONE YOUTH LOST HIS ARM IN THE STRUGGLE, BUT HE CARRIED ON FIGHTING ANYWAY.
THESE BRAVE YOUNG MEN WILLINGLY OFFERED THEIR LIVES AND LIMBS IN THE BATTLE TO DEFEND THEIR FAITH.

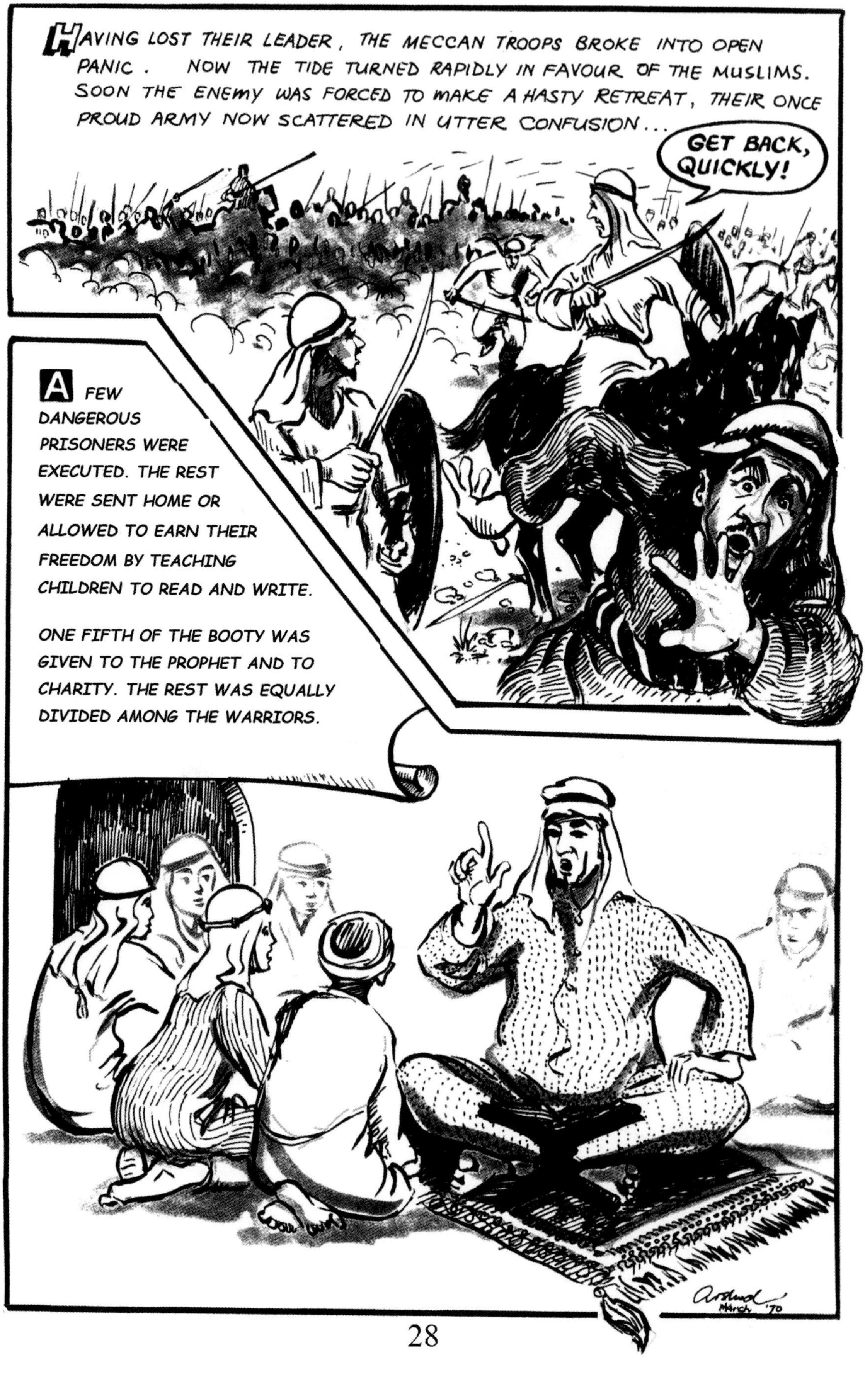
HAVING LOST THEIR LEADER, THE MECCAN TROOPS BROKE INTO OPEN PANIC. NOW THE TIDE TURNED RAPIDLY IN FAVOUR OF THE MUSLIMS. SOON THE ENEMY WAS FORCED TO MAKE A HASTY RETREAT, THEIR ONCE PROUD ARMY NOW SCATTERED IN UTTER CONFUSION...
GET BACK, QUICKLY!
A FEW DANGEROUS PRISONERS WERE EXECUTED. THE REST WERE SENT HOME OR ALLOWED TO EARN THEIR FREEDOM BY TEACHING CHILDREN TO READ AND WRITE.
ONE FIFTH OF THE BOOTY WAS GIVEN TO THE PROPHET AND TO CHARITY. THE REST WAS EQUALLY DIVIDED AMONG THE WARRIORS.

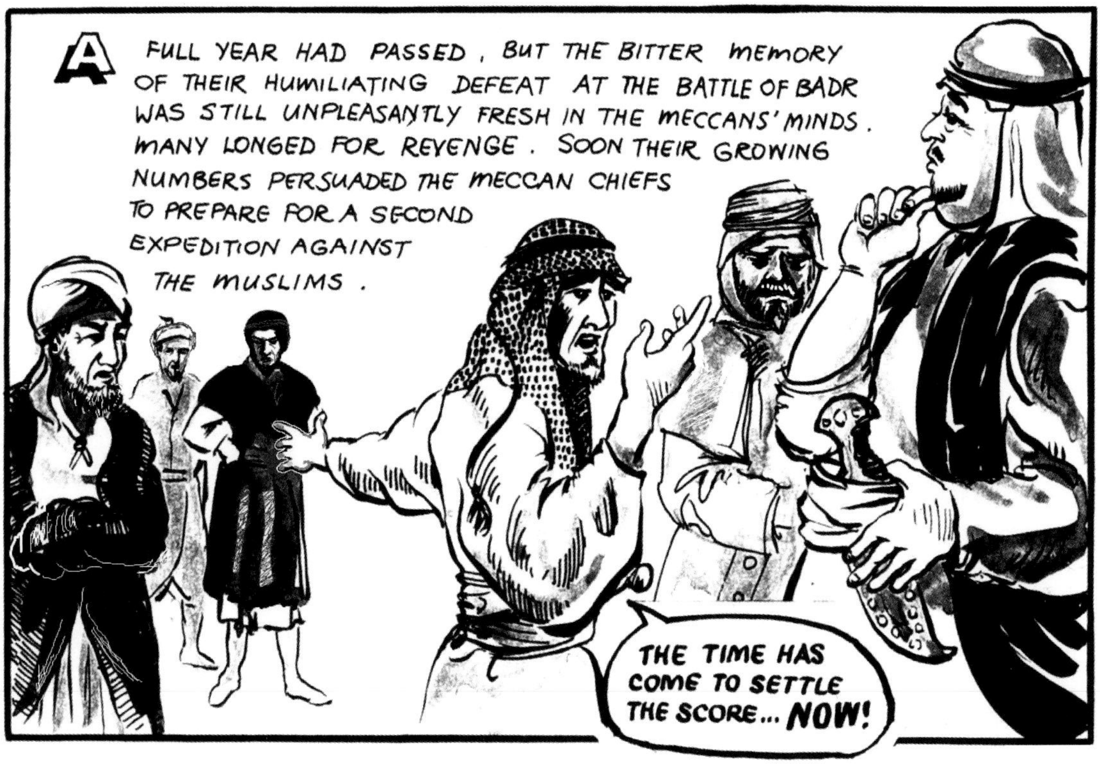
A FULL YEAR HAD PASSED, BUT THE BITTER MEMORY OF THEIR HUMILIATING DEFEAT AT THE BATTLE OF BADR WAS STILL UNPLEASANTLY FRESH IN THE MECCANS' MINDS. MANY LONGED FOR REVENGE. SOON THEIR GROWING NUMBERS PERSUADED THE MECCAN CHIEFS TO PREPARE FOR A SECOND EXPEDITION AGAINST THE MUSLIMS.
THE TIME HAS COME TO SETTLE THE SCORE... NOW!

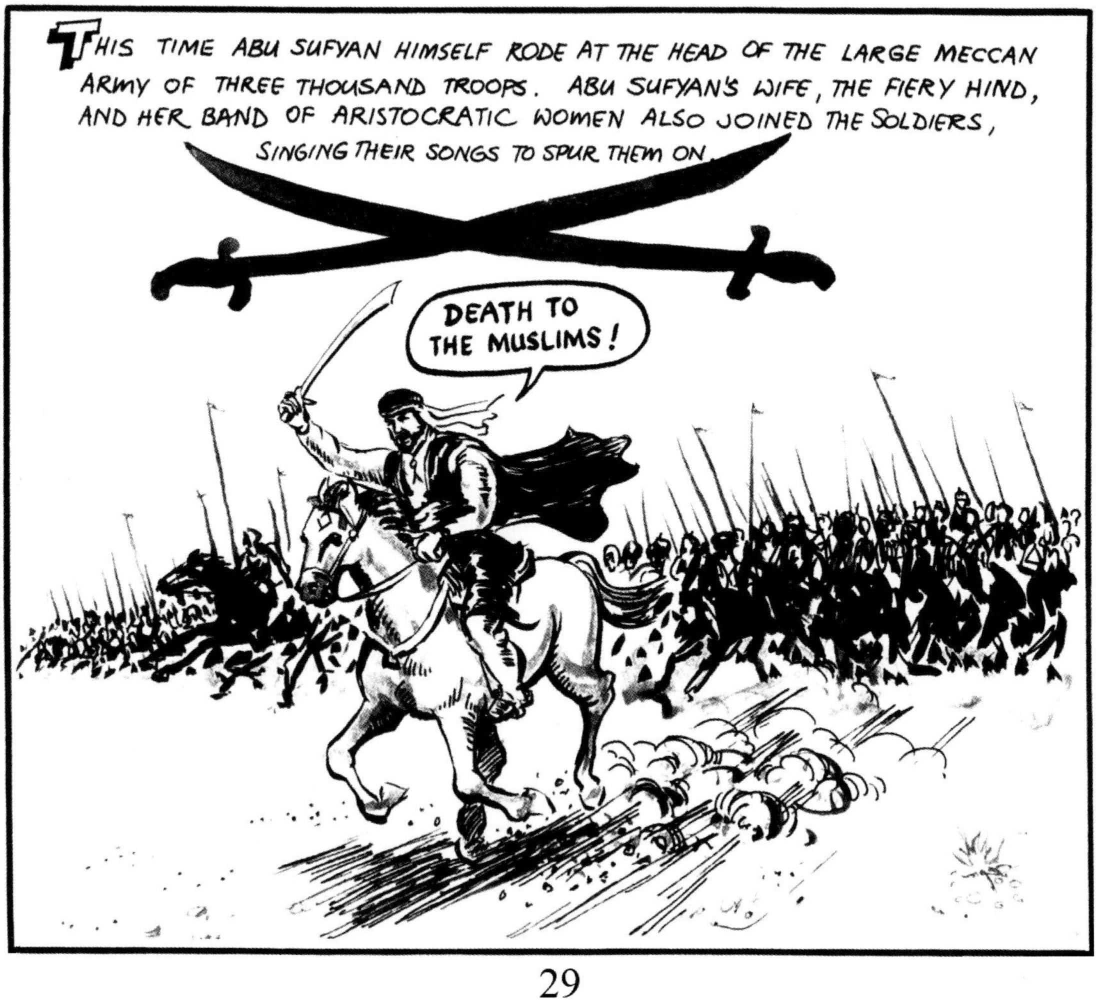
THIS TIME ABU SUFYAN HIMSELF RODE AT THE HEAD OF THE LARGE MECCAN ARMY OF THREE THOUSAND TROOPS. ABU SUFYAN'S WIFE, THE FIERY HIND, AND HER BAND OF ARISTOCRATIC WOMEN ALSO JOINED THE SOLDIERS, SINGING THEIR SONGS TO SPUR THEM ON.
DEATH TO THE MUSLIMS!

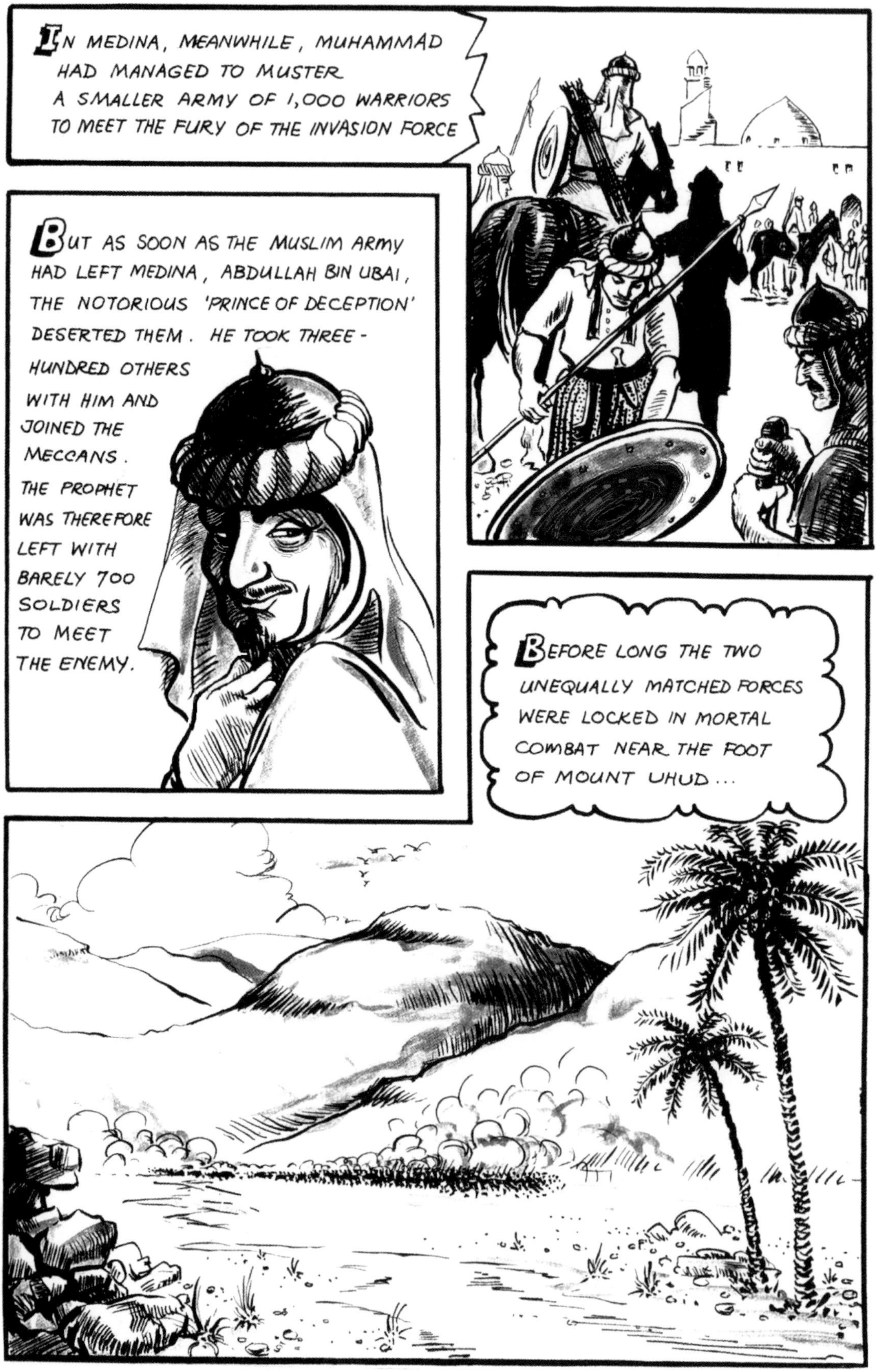
IN MEDINA, MEANWHILE, MUHAMMAD HAD MANAGED TO MUSTER A SMALLER ARMY OF 1,000 WARRIORS TO MEET THE FURY OF THE INVASION FORCE
BUT AS SOON AS THE MUSLIM ARMY HAD LEFT MEDINA, ABDULLAH BIN UBAI, THE NOTORIOUS 'PRINCE OF DECEPTION' DESERTED THEM. HE TOOK THREE-HUNDRED OTHERS WITH HIM AND JOINED THE MECCANS. THE PROPHET WAS THEREFORE LEFT WITH BARELY 700 SOLDIERS TO MEET THE ENEMY.
BEFORE LONG THE TWO UNEQUALLY MATCHED FORCES WERE LOCKED IN MORTAL COMBAT NEAR THE FOOT OF MOUNT UHUD...

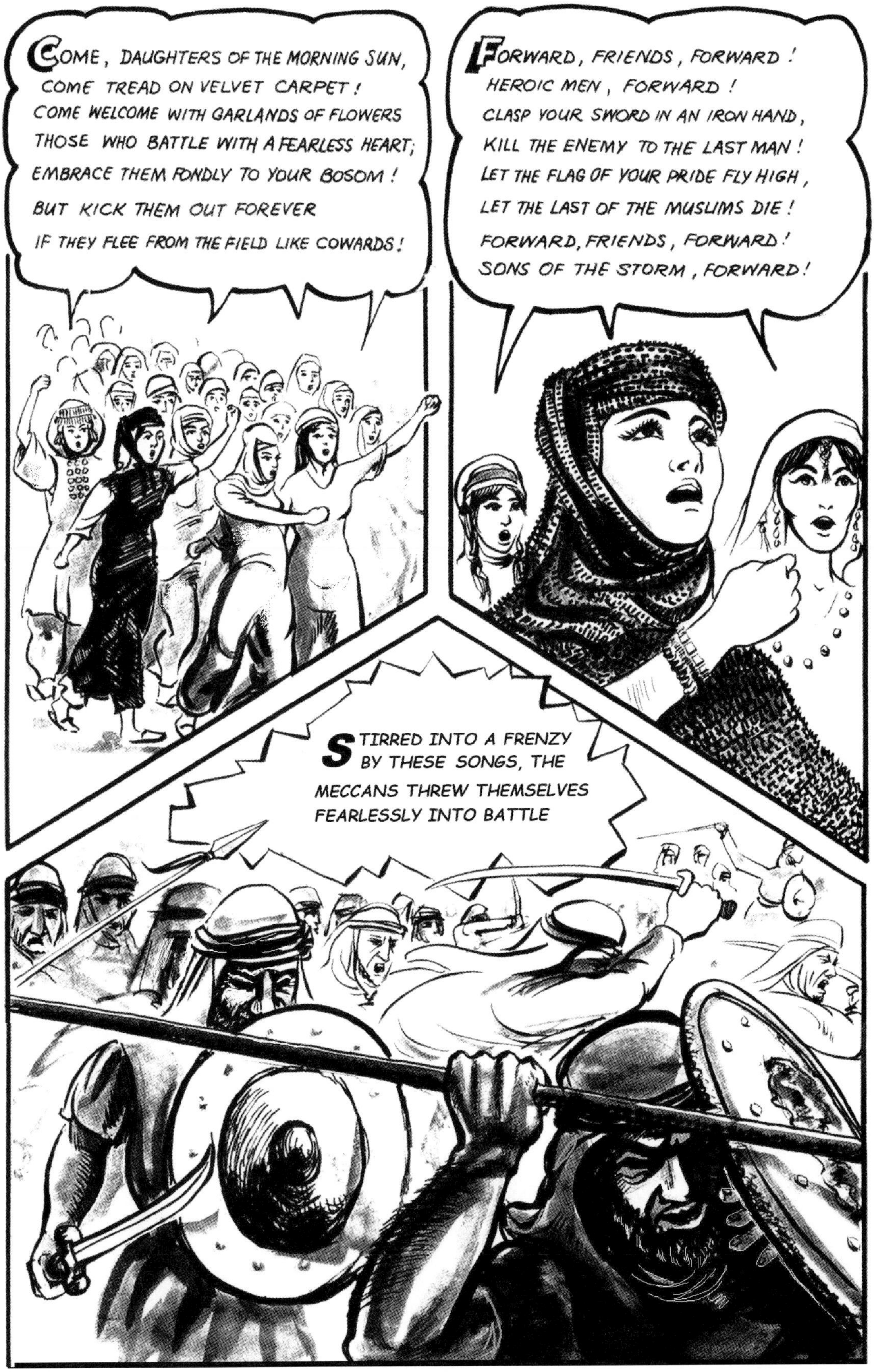
COME, DAUGHTERS OF THE MORNING SUN, COME TREAD ON VELVET CARPET! COME WELCOME WITH GARLANDS OF FLOWERS THOSE WHO BATTLE WITH A FEARLESS HEART; EMBRACE THEM FONDLY TO YOUR BOSOM! BUT KICK THEM OUT FOREVER IF THEY FLEE FROM THE FIELD LIKE COWARDS!
FORWARD, FRIENDS, FORWARD! HEROIC MEN, FORWARD! CLASP YOUR SWORD IN AN IRON HAND, KILL THE ENEMY TO THE LAST MAN! LET THE FLAG OF YOUR PRIDE FLY HIGH, LET THE LAST OF THE MUSLIMS DIE! FORWARD, FRIENDS, FORWARD! SONS OF THE STORM, FORWARD!
STIRRED INTO A FRENZY BY THESE SONGS, THE MECCANS THREW THEMSELVES FEARLESSLY INTO BATTLE

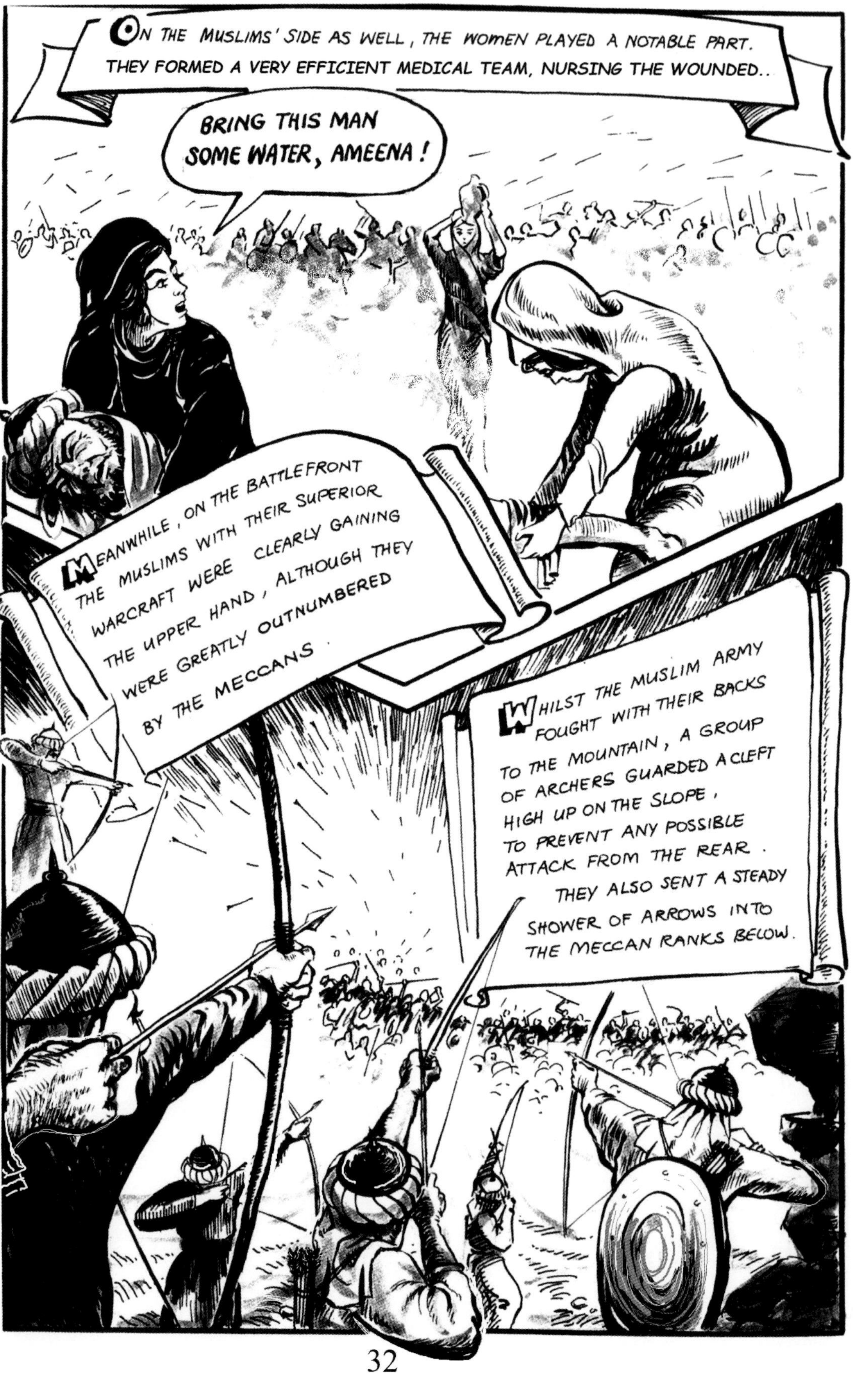
ON THE MUSLIMS' SIDE AS WELL, THE WOMEN PLAYED A NOTABLE PART. THEY FORMED A VERY EFFICIENT MEDICAL TEAM, NURSING THE WOUNDED..
BRING THIS MAN SOME WATER, AMEENA!
MEANWHILE, ON THE BATTLEFRONT THE MUSLIMS WITH THEIR SUPERIOR WARCRAFT WERE CLEARLY GAINING THE UPPER HAND, ALTHOUGH THEY WERE GREATLY OUTNUMBERED BY THE MECCANS.
WHILST THE MUSLIM ARMY FOUGHT WITH THEIR BACKS TO THE MOUNTAIN, A GROUP OF ARCHERS GUARDED A CLEFT HIGH UP ON THE SLOPE, TO PREVENT ANY POSSIBLE ATTACK FROM THE REAR.
THEY ALSO SENT A STEADY SHOWER OF ARROWS INTO THE MECCAN RANKS BELOW.

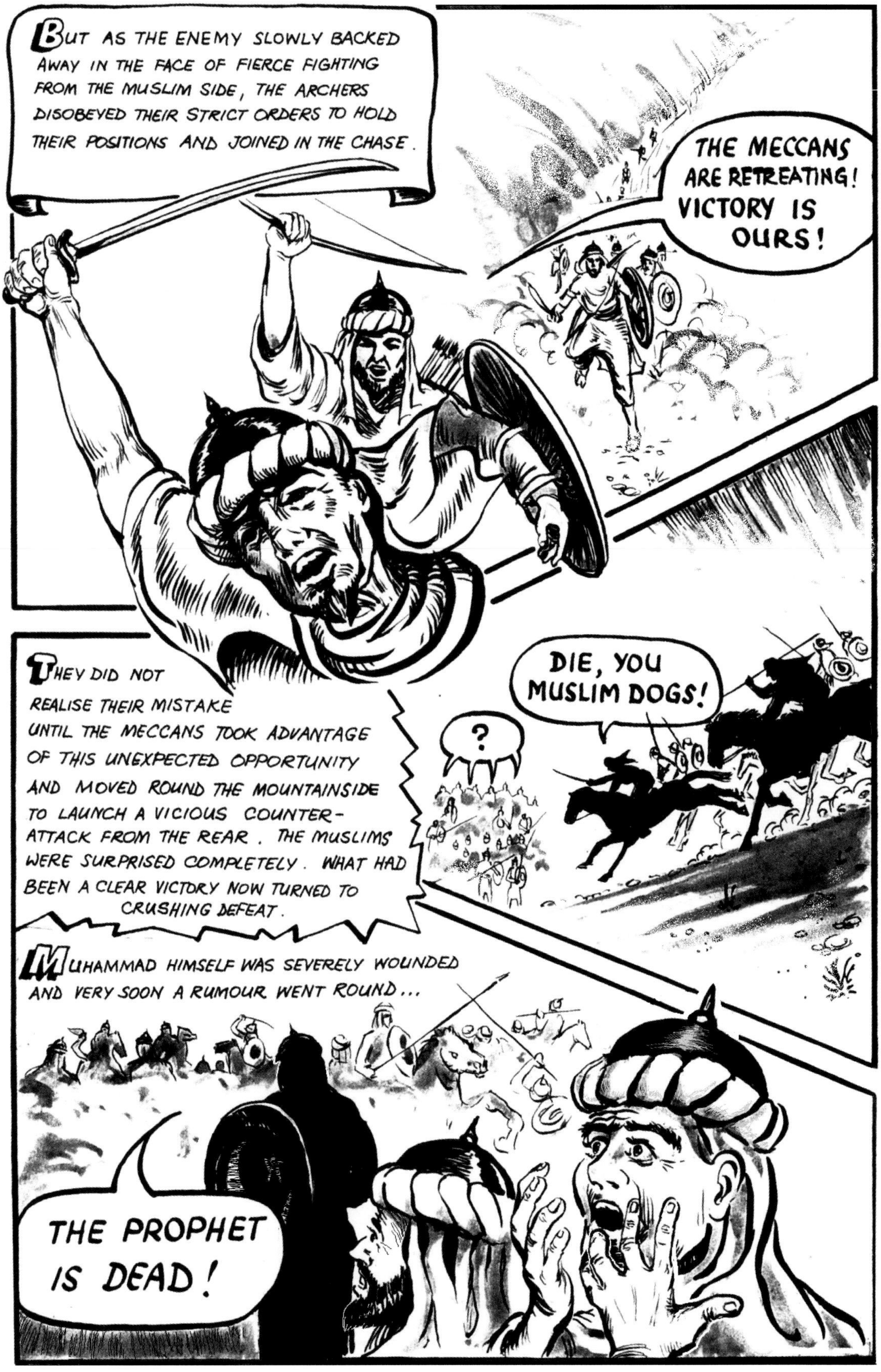

BUT AS THE ENEMY SLOWLY BACKED AWAY IN THE FACE OF FIERCE FIGHTING FROM THE MUSLIM SIDE, THE ARCHERS DISOBEYED THEIR STRICT ORDERS TO HOLD THEIR POSITIONS AND JOINED IN THE CHASE.
THE MECCANS ARE RETREATING! VICTORY IS OURS!
THEY DID NOT REALISE THEIR MISTAKE UNTIL THE MECCANS TOOK ADVANTAGE OF THIS UNEXPECTED OPPORTUNITY AND MOVED ROUND THE MOUNTAINSIDE TO LAUNCH A VICIOUS COUNTER-ATTACK FROM THE REAR. THE MUSLIMS WERE SURPRISED COMPLETELY. WHAT HAD BEEN A CLEAR VICTORY NOW TURNED TO CRUSHING DEFEAT.
?
DIE, YOU MUSLIM DOGS!
MUHAMMAD HIMSELF WAS SEVERELY WOUNDED AND VERY SOON A RUMOUR WENT ROUND...
THE PROPHET IS DEAD!

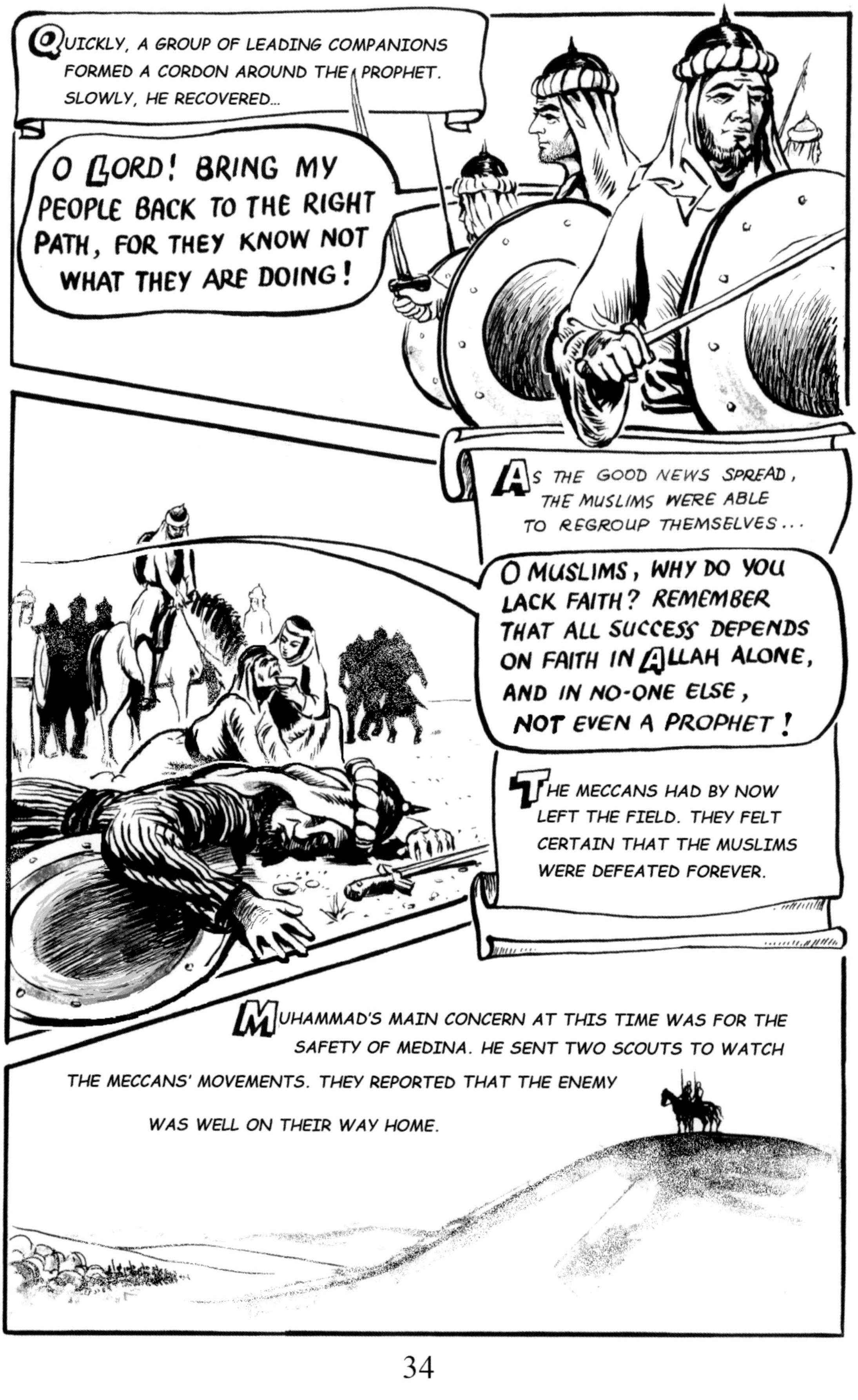
QUICKLY, A GROUP OF LEADING COMPANIONS FORMED A CORDON AROUND THE PROPHET. SLOWLY, HE RECOVERED...
O LORD! BRING MY PEOPLE BACK TO THE RIGHT PATH, FOR THEY KNOW NOT WHAT THEY ARE DOING!
AS THE GOOD NEWS SPREAD, THE MUSLIMS WERE ABLE TO REGROUP THEMSELVES...
O MUSLIMS, WHY DO YOU LACK FAITH? REMEMBER THAT ALL SUCCESS DEPENDS ON FAITH IN ALLAH ALONE, AND IN NO-ONE ELSE, NOT EVEN A PROPHET!
THE MECCANS HAD BY NOW LEFT THE FIELD. THEY FELT CERTAIN THAT THE MUSLIMS WERE DEFEATED FOREVER.
MUHAMMAD'S MAIN CONCERN AT THIS TIME WAS FOR THE SAFETY OF MEDINA. HE SENT TWO SCOUTS TO WATCH THE MECCANS' MOVEMENTS. THEY REPORTED THAT THE ENEMY WAS WELL ON THEIR WAY HOME.

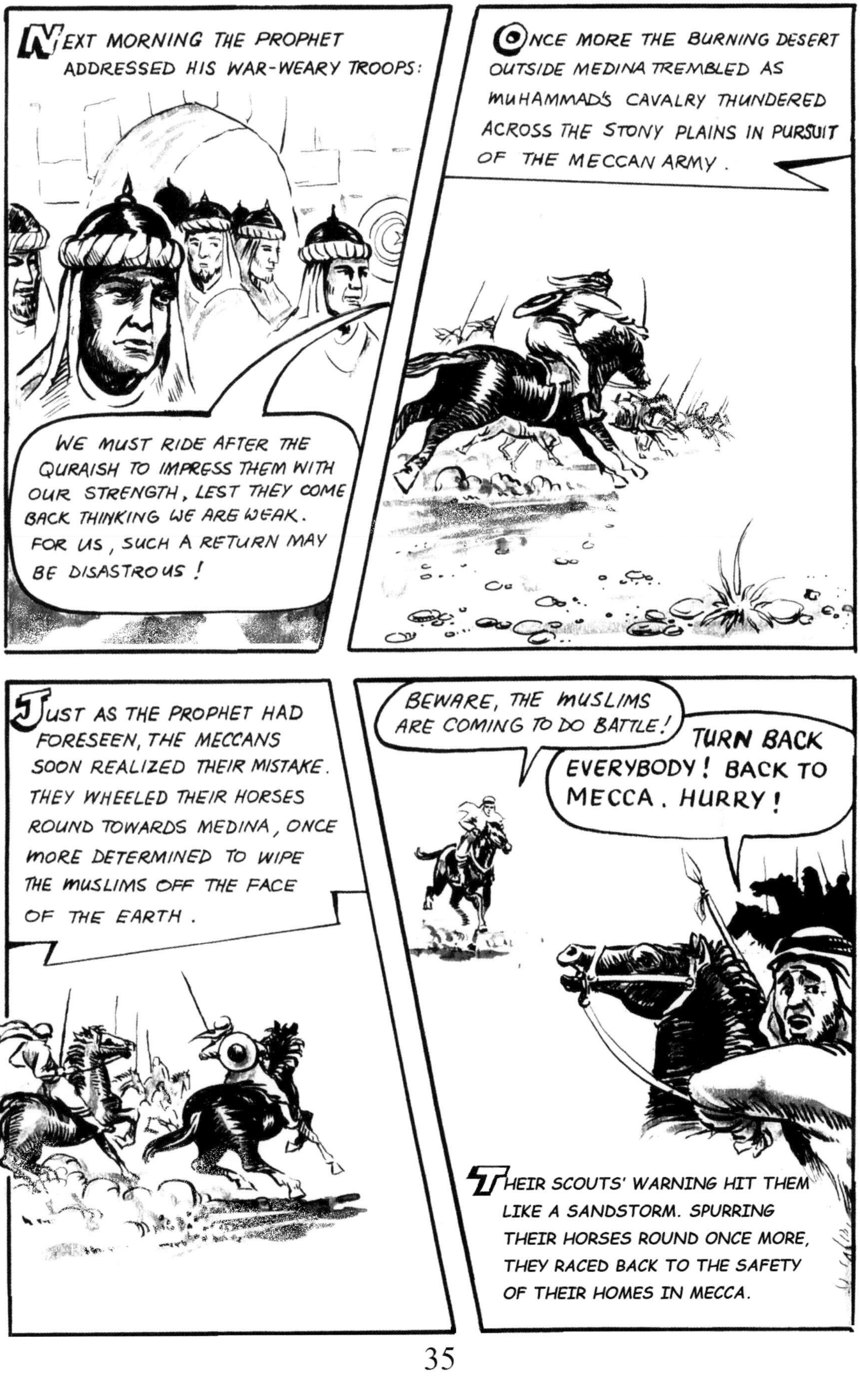
NEXT MORNING THE PROPHET ADDRESSED HIS WAR-WEARY TROOPS:
WE MUST RIDE AFTER THE QURAISH TO IMPRESS THEM WITH OUR STRENGTH, LEST THEY COME BACK THINKING WE ARE WEAK. FOR US, SUCH A RETURN MAY BE DISASTROUS!
ONCE MORE THE BURNING DESERT OUTSIDE MEDINA TREMBLED AS MUHAMMAD'S CAVALRY THUNDERED ACROSS THE STONY PLAINS IN PURSUIT OF THE MECCAN ARMY.
JUST AS THE PROPHET HAD FORESEEN, THE MECCANS SOON REALIZED THEIR MISTAKE. THEY WHEELED THEIR HORSES ROUND TOWARDS MEDINA, ONCE MORE DETERMINED TO WIPE THE MUSLIMS OFF THE FACE OF THE EARTH.
BEWARE, THE MUSLIMS ARE COMING TO DO BATTLE!
TURN BACK EVERYBODY! BACK TO MECCA. HURRY!
THEIR SCOUTS' WARNING HIT THEM LIKE A SANDSTORM. SPURRING THEIR HORSES ROUND ONCE MORE, THEY RACED BACK TO THE SAFETY OF THEIR HOMES IN MECCA.

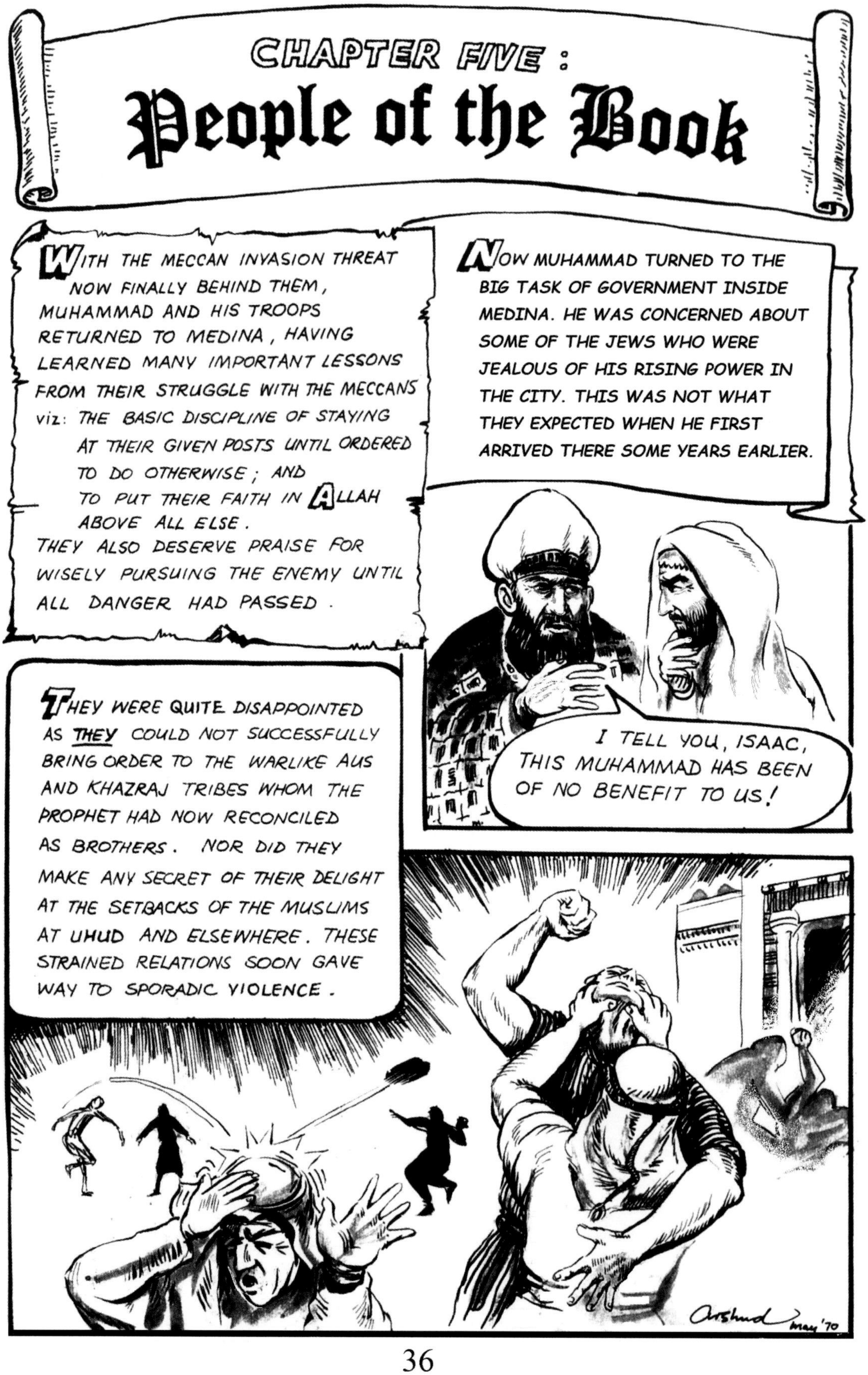
CHAPTER FIVE :
People of the Book
WITH THE MECCAN INVASION THREAT NOW FINALLY BEHIND THEM, MUHAMMAD AND HIS TROOPS RETURNED TO MEDINA, HAVING LEARNED MANY IMPORTANT LESSONS FROM THEIR STRUGGLE WITH THE MECCANS viz: THE BASIC DISCIPLINE OF STAYING AT THEIR GIVEN POSTS UNTIL ORDERED TO DO OTHERWISE; AND TO PUT THEIR FAITH IN ALLAH ABOVE ALL ELSE. THEY ALSO DESERVE PRAISE FOR WISELY PURSUING THE ENEMY UNTIL ALL DANGER HAD PASSED.
NOW MUHAMMAD TURNED TO THE BIG TASK OF GOVERNMENT INSIDE MEDINA. HE WAS CONCERNED ABOUT SOME OF THE JEWS WHO WERE JEALOUS OF HIS RISING POWER IN THE CITY. THIS WAS NOT WHAT THEY EXPECTED WHEN HE FIRST ARRIVED THERE SOME YEARS EARLIER.
I TELL YOU, ISAAC, THIS MUHAMMAD HAS BEEN OF NO BENEFIT TO US!
THEY WERE QUITE DISAPPOINTED AS THEY COULD NOT SUCCESSFULLY BRING ORDER TO THE WARLIKE AUS AND KHAZRAJ TRIBES WHOM THE PROPHET HAD NOW RECONCILED AS BROTHERS. NOR DID THEY MAKE ANY SECRET OF THEIR DELIGHT AT THE SETBACKS OF THE MUSLIMS AT UHUD AND ELSEWHERE. THESE STRAINED RELATIONS SOON GAVE WAY TO SPORADIC VIOLENCE.
Arshad may '70

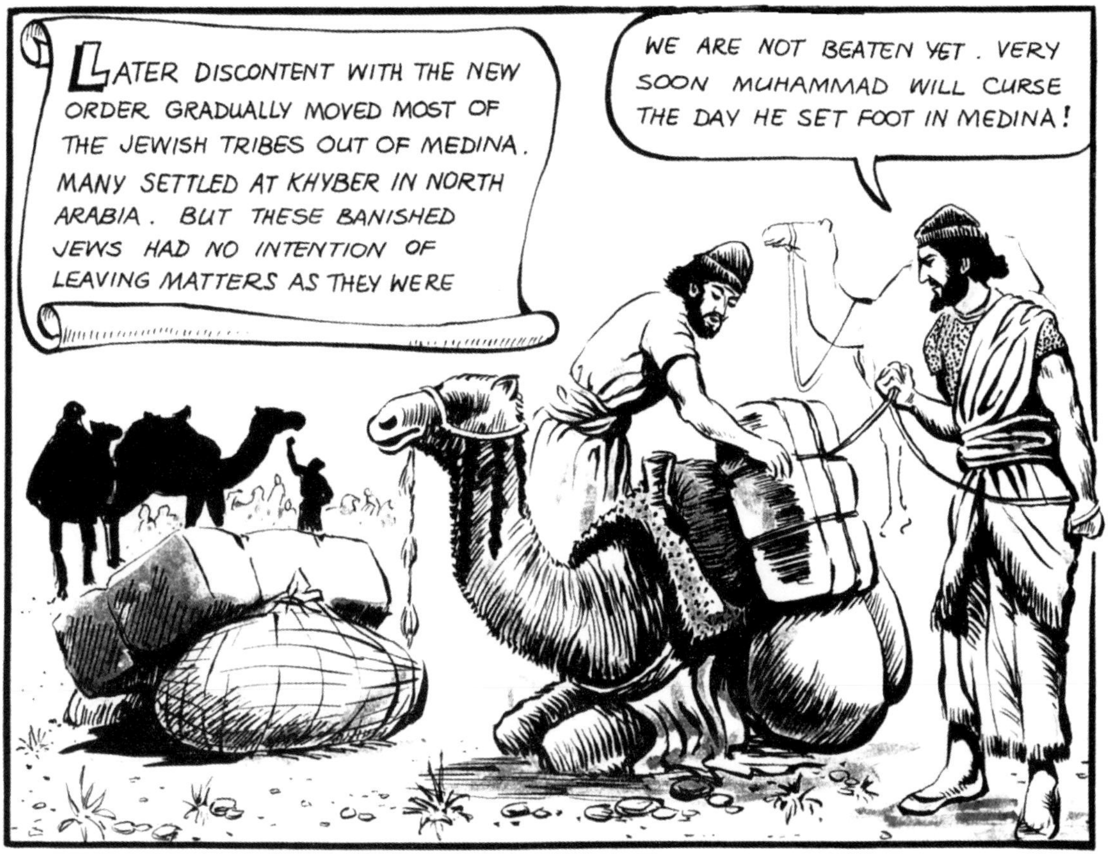
LATER DISCONTENT WITH THE NEW ORDER GRADUALLY MOVED MOST OF THE JEWISH TRIBES OUT OF MEDINA. MANY SETTLED AT KHYBER IN NORTH ARABIA. BUT THESE BANISHED JEWS HAD NO INTENTION OF LEAVING MATTERS AS THEY WERE
WE ARE NOT BEATEN YET. VERY SOON MUHAMMAD WILL CURSE THE DAY HE SET FOOT IN MEDINA!

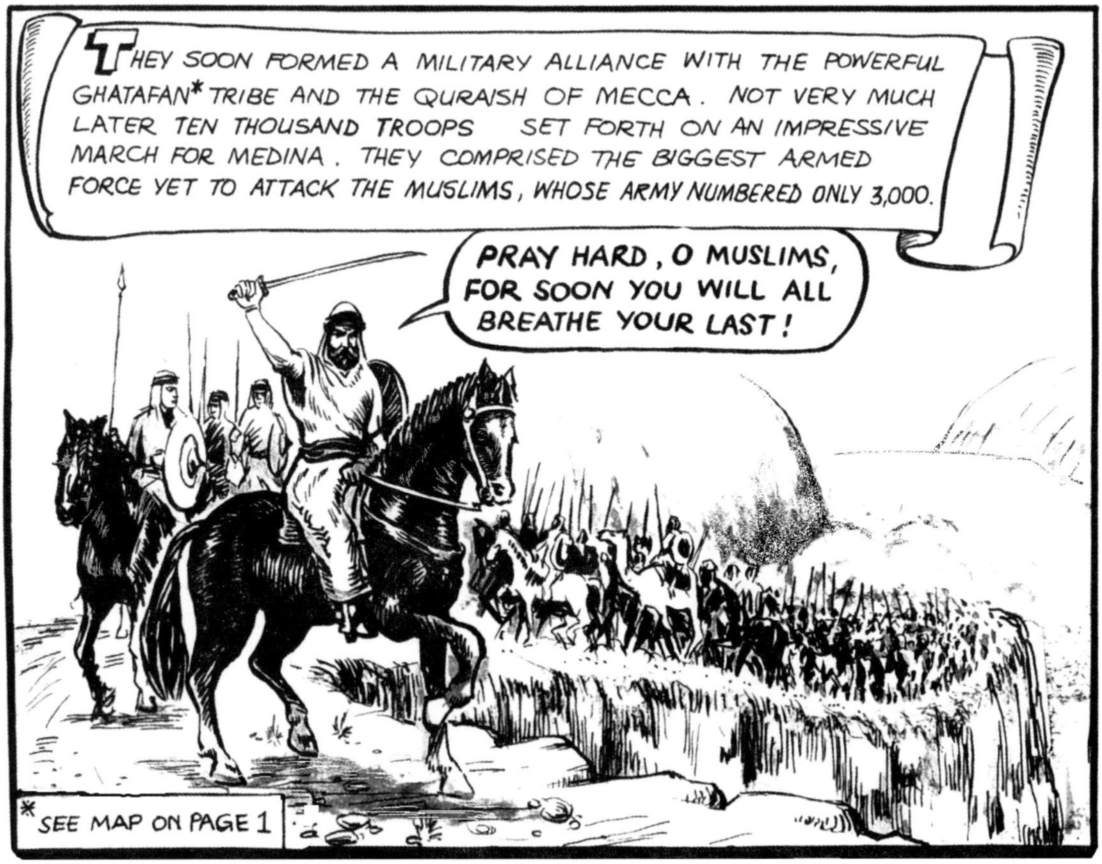
THEY SOON FORMED A MILITARY ALLIANCE WITH THE POWERFUL GHATAFAN* TRIBE AND THE QURAISH OF MECCA. NOT VERY MUCH LATER TEN THOUSAND TROOPS SET FORTH ON AN IMPRESSIVE MARCH FOR MEDINA. THEY COMPRISED THE BIGGEST ARMED FORCE YET TO ATTACK THE MUSLIMS, WHOSE ARMY NUMBERED ONLY 3,000.
PRAY HARD, O MUSLIMS, FOR SOON YOU WILL ALL BREATHE YOUR LAST!
*SEE MAP ON PAGE 1

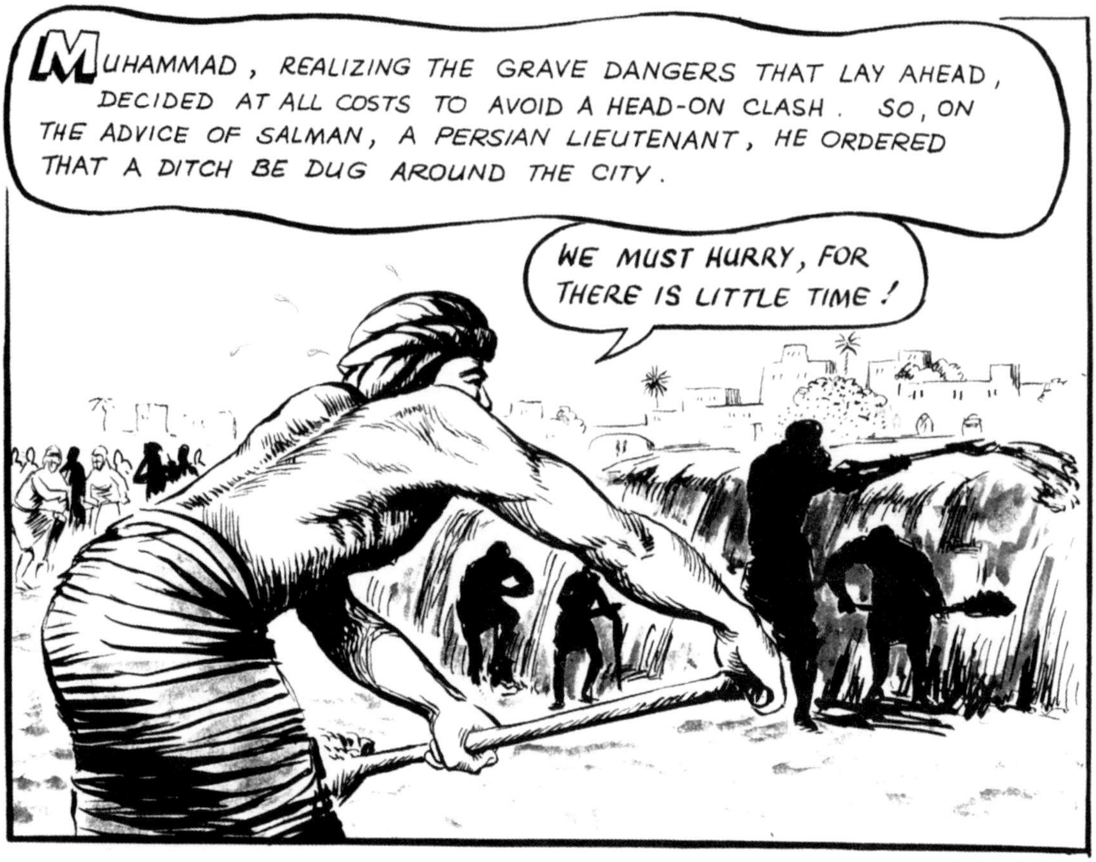
MUHAMMAD, REALIZING THE GRAVE DANGERS THAT LAY AHEAD, DECIDED AT ALL COSTS TO AVOID A HEAD-ON CLASH. SO, ON THE ADVICE OF SALMAN, A PERSIAN LIEUTENANT, HE ORDERED THAT A DITCH BE DUG AROUND THE CITY.
WE MUST HURRY, FOR THERE IS LITTLE TIME!

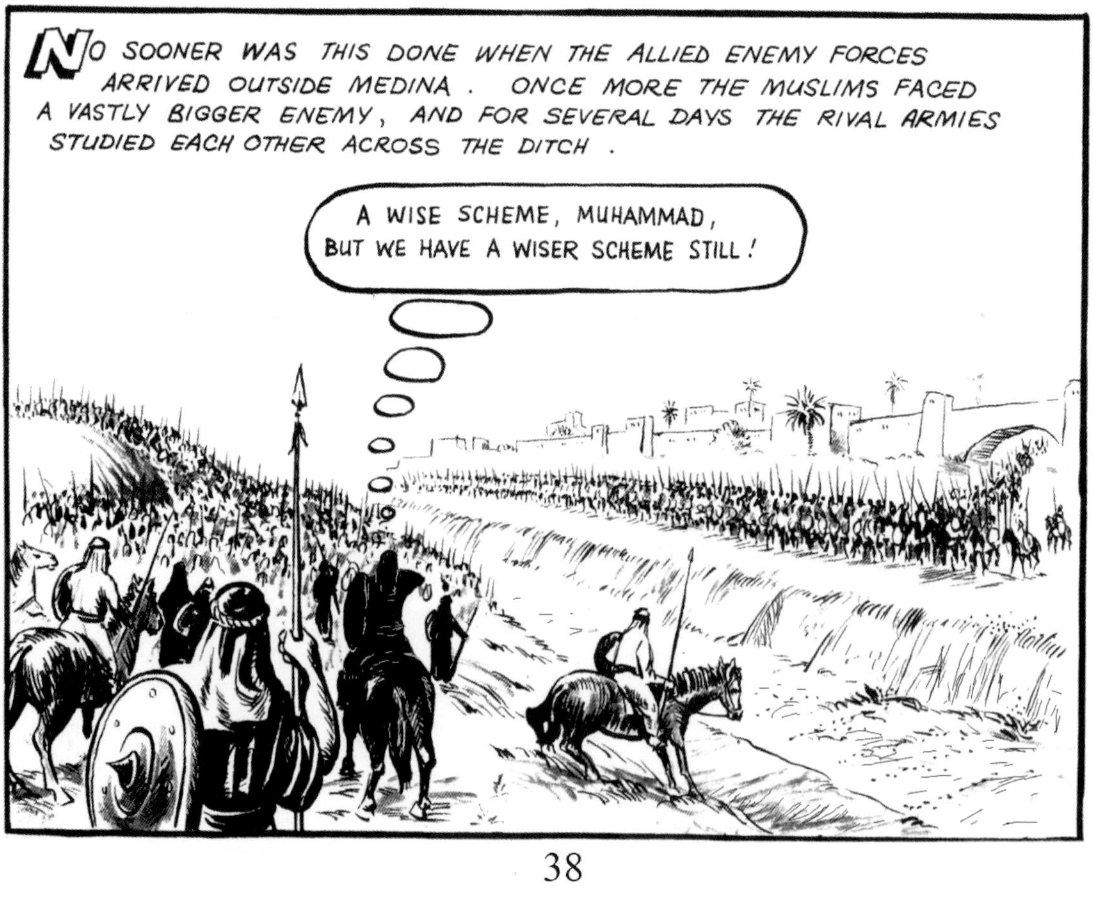
NO SOONER WAS THIS DONE WHEN THE ALLIED ENEMY FORCES ARRIVED OUTSIDE MEDINA. ONCE MORE THE MUSLIMS FACED A VASTLY BIGGER ENEMY, AND FOR SEVERAL DAYS THE RIVAL ARMIES STUDIED EACH OTHER ACROSS THE DITCH.
A WISE SCHEME, MUHAMMAD, BUT WE HAVE A WISER SCHEME STILL!

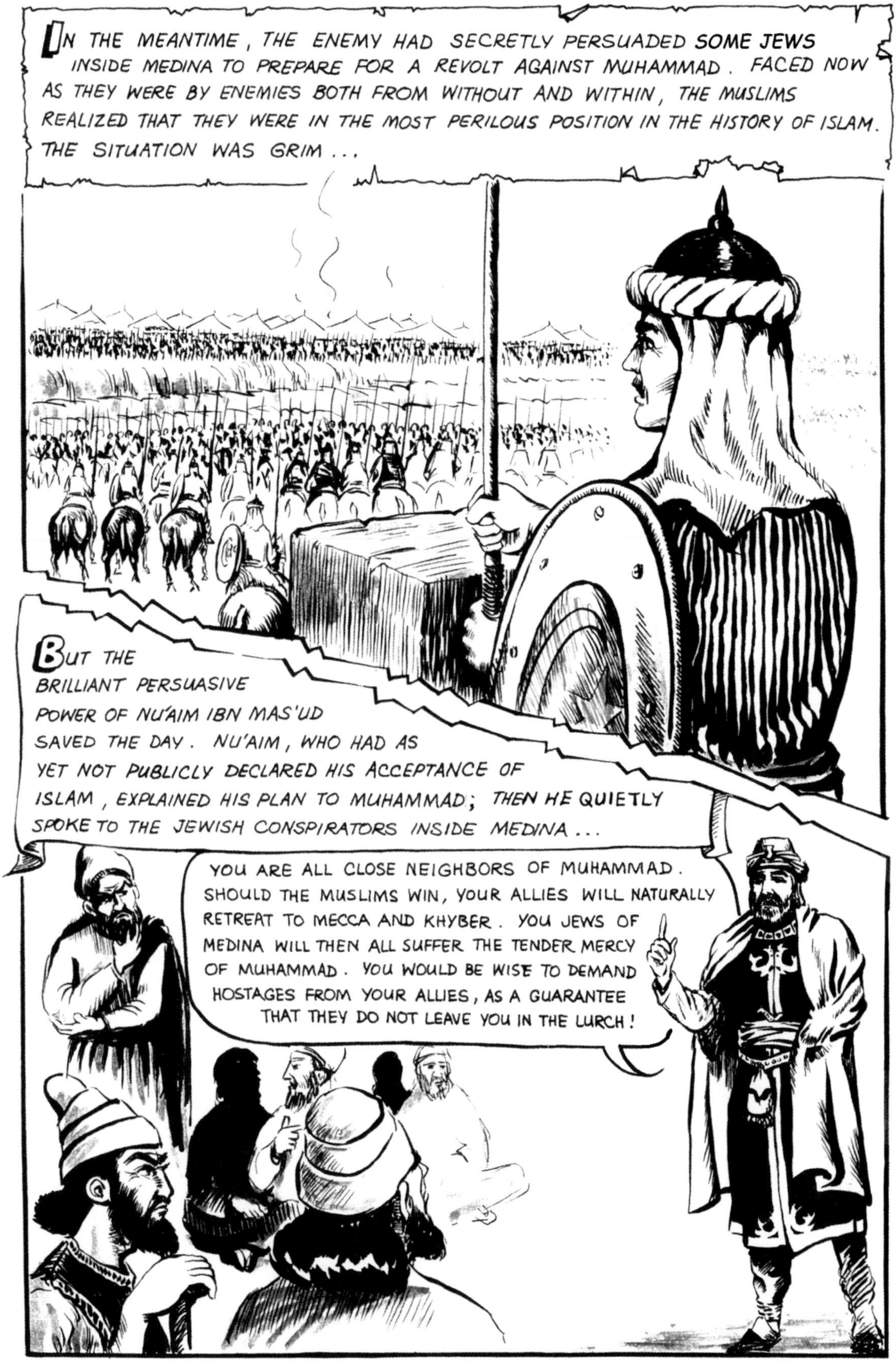
IN THE MEANTIME, THE ENEMY HAD SECRETLY PERSUADED SOME JEWS INSIDE MEDINA TO PREPARE FOR A REVOLT AGAINST MUHAMMAD. FACED NOW AS THEY WERE BY ENEMIES BOTH FROM WITHOUT AND WITHIN, THE MUSLIMS REALIZED THAT THEY WERE IN THE MOST PERILOUS POSITION IN THE HISTORY OF ISLAM. THE SITUATION WAS GRIM ...
BUT THE BRILLIANT PERSUASIVE POWER OF NU'AIM IBN MAS'UD SAVED THE DAY. NU'AIM, WHO HAD AS YET NOT PUBLICLY DECLARED HIS ACCEPTANCE OF ISLAM, EXPLAINED HIS PLAN TO MUHAMMAD; THEN HE QUIETLY SPOKE TO THE JEWISH CONSPIRATORS INSIDE MEDINA ...
YOU ARE ALL CLOSE NEIGHBORS OF MUHAMMAD. SHOULD THE MUSLIMS WIN, YOUR ALLIES WILL NATURALLY RETREAT TO MECCA AND KHYBER. YOU JEWS OF MEDINA WILL THEN ALL SUFFER THE TENDER MERCY OF MUHAMMAD. YOU WOULD BE WISE TO DEMAND HOSTAGES FROM YOUR ALLIES, AS A GUARANTEE THAT THEY DO NOT LEAVE YOU IN THE LURCH!

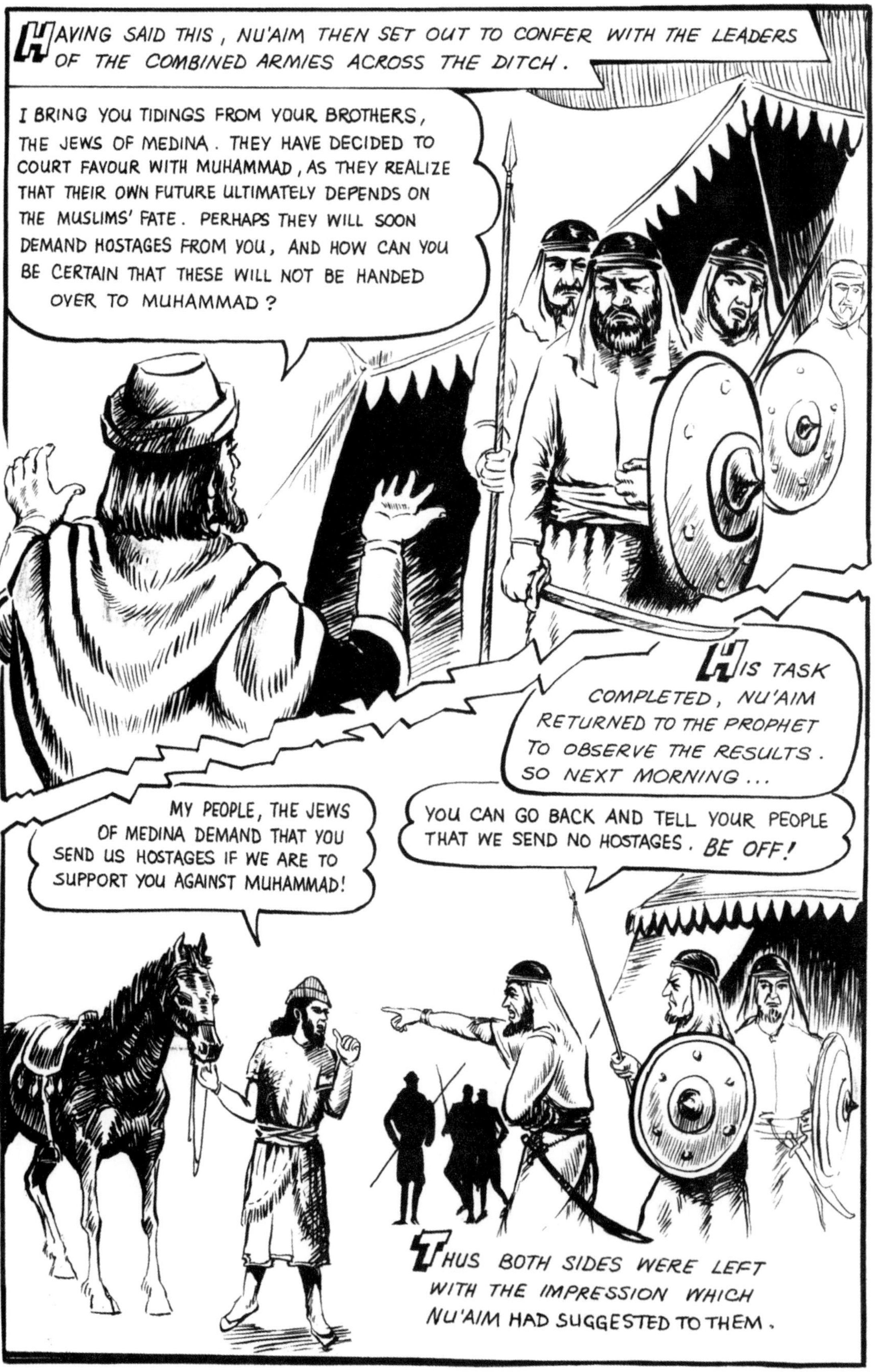
HAVING SAID THIS, NU'AIM THEN SET OUT TO CONFER WITH THE LEADERS OF THE COMBINED ARMIES ACROSS THE DITCH.
I BRING YOU TIDINGS FROM YOUR BROTHERS, THE JEWS OF MEDINA. THEY HAVE DECIDED TO COURT FAVOUR WITH MUHAMMAD, AS THEY REALIZE THAT THEIR OWN FUTURE ULTIMATELY DEPENDS ON THE MUSLIMS' FATE. PERHAPS THEY WILL SOON DEMAND HOSTAGES FROM YOU, AND HOW CAN YOU BE CERTAIN THAT THESE WILL NOT BE HANDED OVER TO MUHAMMAD?
HIS TASK COMPLETED, NU'AIM RETURNED TO THE PROPHET TO OBSERVE THE RESULTS. SO NEXT MORNING...
MY PEOPLE, THE JEWS OF MEDINA DEMAND THAT YOU SEND US HOSTAGES IF WE ARE TO SUPPORT YOU AGAINST MUHAMMAD!
YOU CAN GO BACK AND TELL YOUR PEOPLE THAT WE SEND NO HOSTAGES. BE OFF!
THUS BOTH SIDES WERE LEFT WITH THE IMPRESSION WHICH NU'AIM HAD SUGGESTED TO THEM.

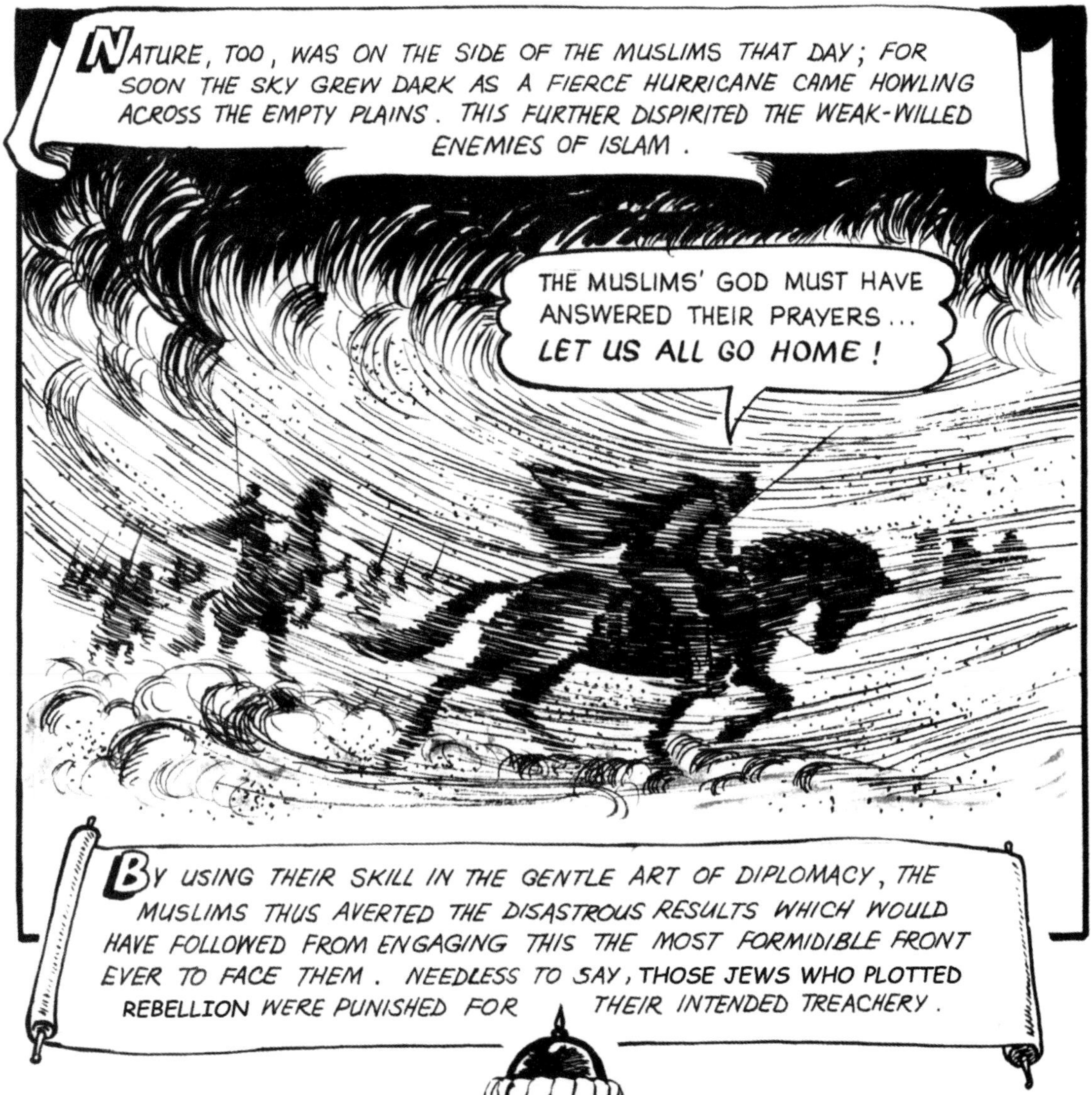
NATURE, TOO, WAS ON THE SIDE OF THE MUSLIMS THAT DAY; FOR SOON THE SKY GREW DARK AS A FIERCE HURRICANE CAME HOWLING ACROSS THE EMPTY PLAINS. THIS FURTHER DISPIRITED THE WEAK-WILLED ENEMIES OF ISLAM.
THE MUSLIMS' GOD MUST HAVE ANSWERED THEIR PRAYERS... LET US ALL GO HOME!
BY USING THEIR SKILL IN THE GENTLE ART OF DIPLOMACY, THE MUSLIMS THUS AVERTED THE DISASTROUS RESULTS WHICH WOULD HAVE FOLLOWED FROM ENGAGING THIS THE MOST FORMIDIBLE FRONT EVER TO FACE THEM. NEEDLESS TO SAY, THOSE JEWS WHO PLOTTED REBELLION WERE PUNISHED FOR THEIR INTENDED TREACHERY.

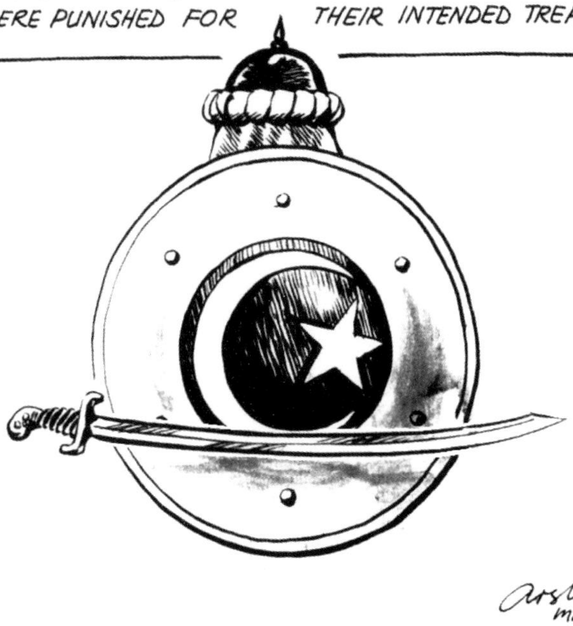

Rabbi Muhayriq

Not all Jews regarded Muslims as enemies. Some of the Jews of Medina were loyal to Prophet Muhammad sws and they even fought alongside him in the Battle of Uhud.

Rabbi Muhayriq, a learned and respected scholar, became the first Jewish martyr in Islam. He fought and died alongside the Muslims defending Medina. Before his death, he had bequeathed his date gardens and weapons to the Prophet sws. After his death, these gardens became the first Waqf (property held in Trust for the benefit of all citizens).

Prophet Muhammad sws described Rabbi Muhayriq as **"The Best of the Jews."**

Reference: Ibn Hisham, al-Sira al-Nabawiyya, vol. 1 (Cairo, 1955) p. 518.

CHAPTER SIX:
The Conquest of Mecca

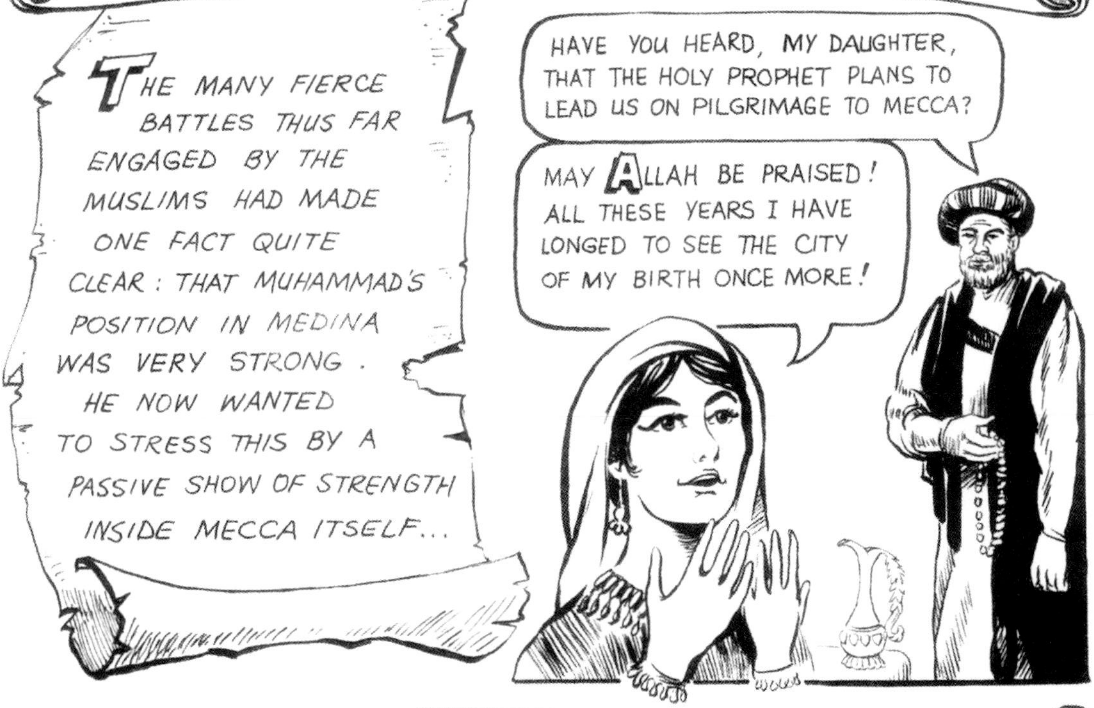
THE MANY FIERCE BATTLES THUS FAR ENGAGED BY THE MUSLIMS HAD MADE ONE FACT QUITE CLEAR: THAT MUHAMMAD'S POSITION IN MEDINA WAS VERY STRONG. HE NOW WANTED TO STRESS THIS BY A PASSIVE SHOW OF STRENGTH INSIDE MECCA ITSELF...
HAVE YOU HEARD, MY DAUGHTER, THAT THE HOLY PROPHET PLANS TO LEAD US ON PILGRIMAGE TO MECCA?
MAY ALLAH BE PRAISED! ALL THESE YEARS I HAVE LONGED TO SEE THE CITY OF MY BIRTH ONCE MORE!

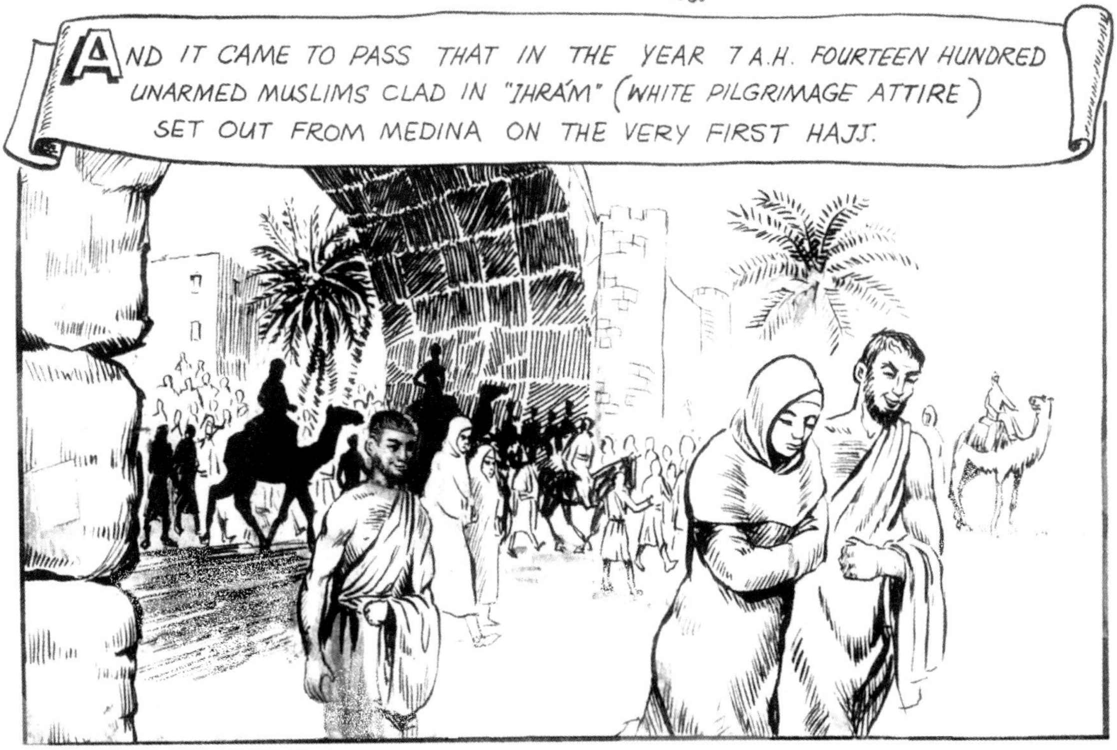
AND IT CAME TO PASS THAT IN THE YEAR 7 A.H. FOURTEEN HUNDRED UNARMED MUSLIMS CLAD IN "IHRÁM" (WHITE PILGRIMAGE ATTIRE) SET OUT FROM MEDINA ON THE VERY FIRST HAJJ.

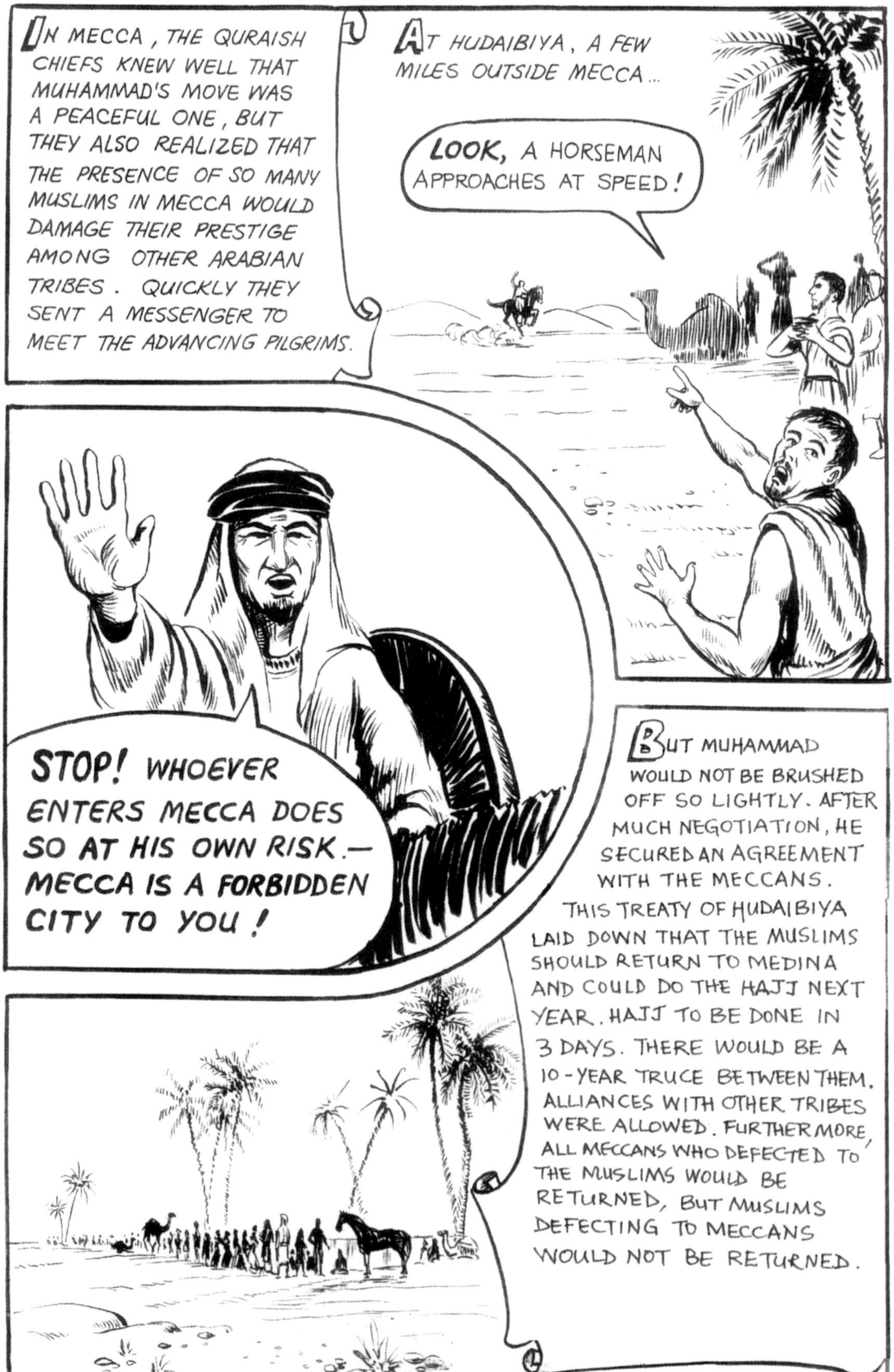
IN MECCA, THE QURAISH CHIEFS KNEW WELL THAT MUHAMMAD'S MOVE WAS A PEACEFUL ONE, BUT THEY ALSO REALIZED THAT THE PRESENCE OF SO MANY MUSLIMS IN MECCA WOULD DAMAGE THEIR PRESTIGE AMONG OTHER ARABIAN TRIBES. QUICKLY THEY SENT A MESSENGER TO MEET THE ADVANCING PILGRIMS.
AT HUDAIBIYA, A FEW MILES OUTSIDE MECCA...
LOOK, A HORSEMAN APPROACHES AT SPEED!
STOP! WHOEVER ENTERS MECCA DOES SO AT HIS OWN RISK.— MECCA IS A FORBIDDEN CITY TO YOU!
BUT MUHAMMAD WOULD NOT BE BRUSHED OFF SO LIGHTLY. AFTER MUCH NEGOTIATION, HE SECURED AN AGREEMENT WITH THE MECCANS.
THIS TREATY OF HUDAIBIYA LAID DOWN THAT THE MUSLIMS SHOULD RETURN TO MEDINA AND COULD DO THE HAJJ NEXT YEAR. HAJJ TO BE DONE IN 3 DAYS. THERE WOULD BE A 10-YEAR TRUCE BETWEEN THEM. ALLIANCES WITH OTHER TRIBES WERE ALLOWED. FURTHERMORE, ALL MECCANS WHO DEFECTED TO THE MUSLIMS WOULD BE RETURNED, BUT MUSLIMS DEFECTING TO MECCANS WOULD NOT BE RETURNED.

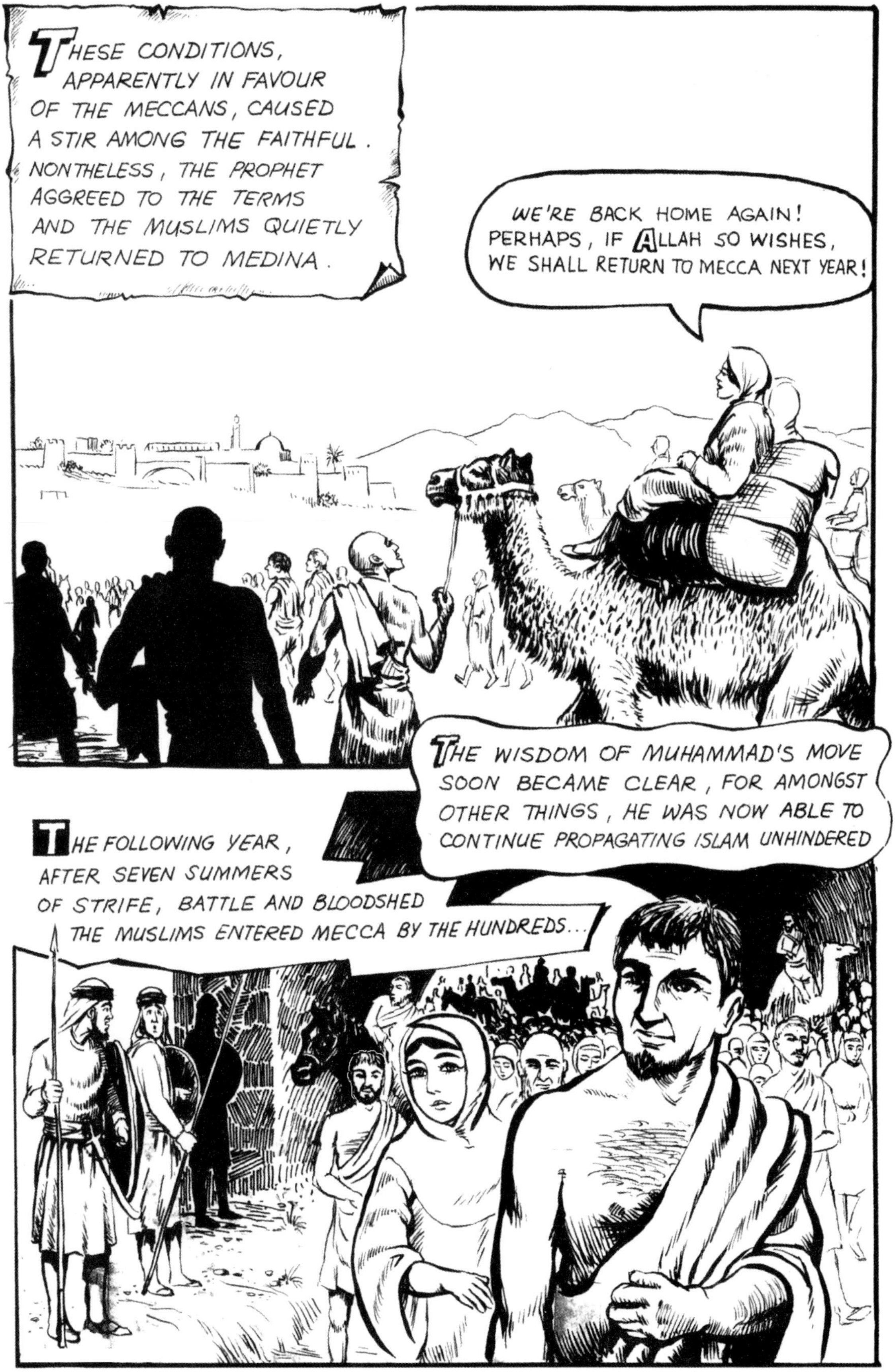
THESE CONDITIONS, APPARENTLY IN FAVOUR OF THE MECCANS, CAUSED A STIR AMONG THE FAITHFUL. NONTHELESS, THE PROPHET AGGREED TO THE TERMS AND THE MUSLIMS QUIETLY RETURNED TO MEDINA.
WE'RE BACK HOME AGAIN! PERHAPS, IF ALLAH SO WISHES, WE SHALL RETURN TO MECCA NEXT YEAR!
THE WISDOM OF MUHAMMAD'S MOVE SOON BECAME CLEAR, FOR AMONGST OTHER THINGS, HE WAS NOW ABLE TO CONTINUE PROPAGATING ISLAM UNHINDERED
THE FOLLOWING YEAR, AFTER SEVEN SUMMERS OF STRIFE, BATTLE AND BLOODSHED THE MUSLIMS ENTERED MECCA BY THE HUNDREDS...

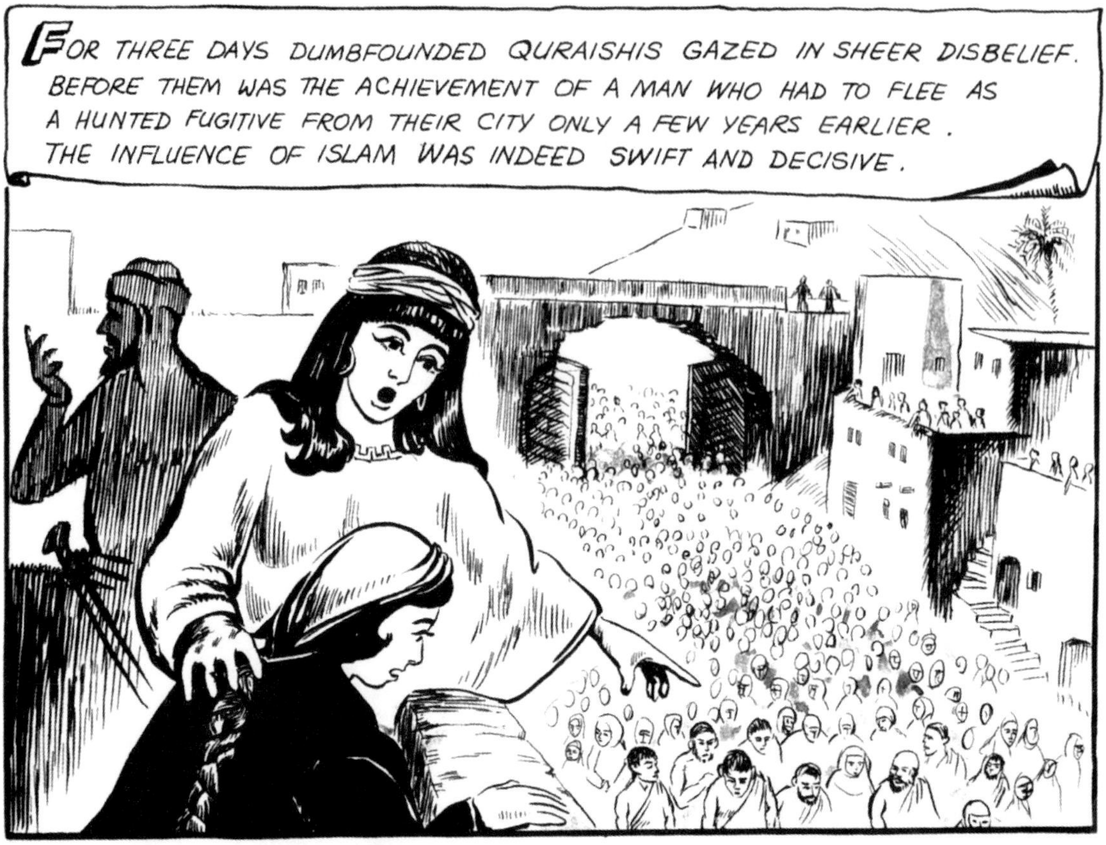
FOR THREE DAYS DUMBFOUNDED QURAISHIS GAZED IN SHEER DISBELIEF. BEFORE THEM WAS THE ACHIEVEMENT OF A MAN WHO HAD TO FLEE AS A HUNTED FUGITIVE FROM THEIR CITY ONLY A FEW YEARS EARLIER . THE INFLUENCE OF ISLAM WAS INDEED SWIFT AND DECISIVE .

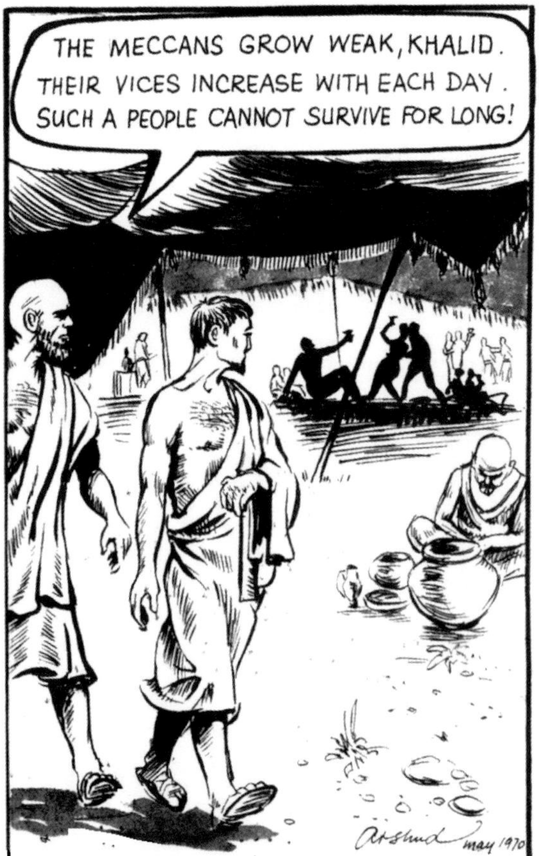
THE MECCANS GROW WEAK, KHALID. THEIR VICES INCREASE WITH EACH DAY . SUCH A PEOPLE CANNOT SURVIVE FOR LONG!
Arshad may 1970

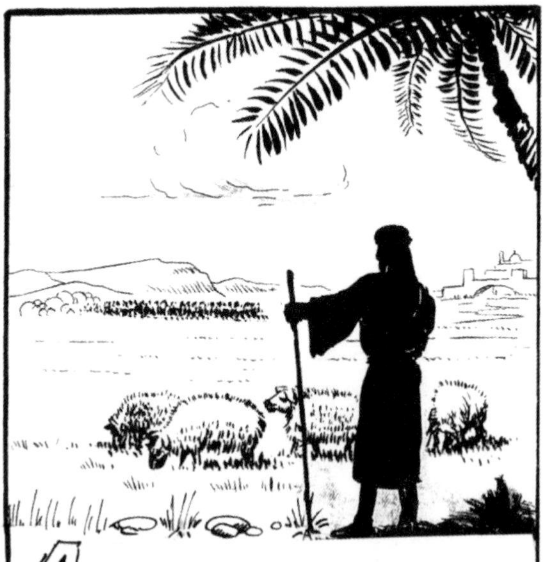
AFTER COMPLETING THEIR FIRST PILGRIMAGE TO MECCA, THE HAJJ, THE MUSLIMS RETURNED SAFELY TO MEDINA. NOW PROPHET MUHAMMAD COULD START TO BUILD RELATIONS WITH OTHER TRIBES BEYOND HIS CITY

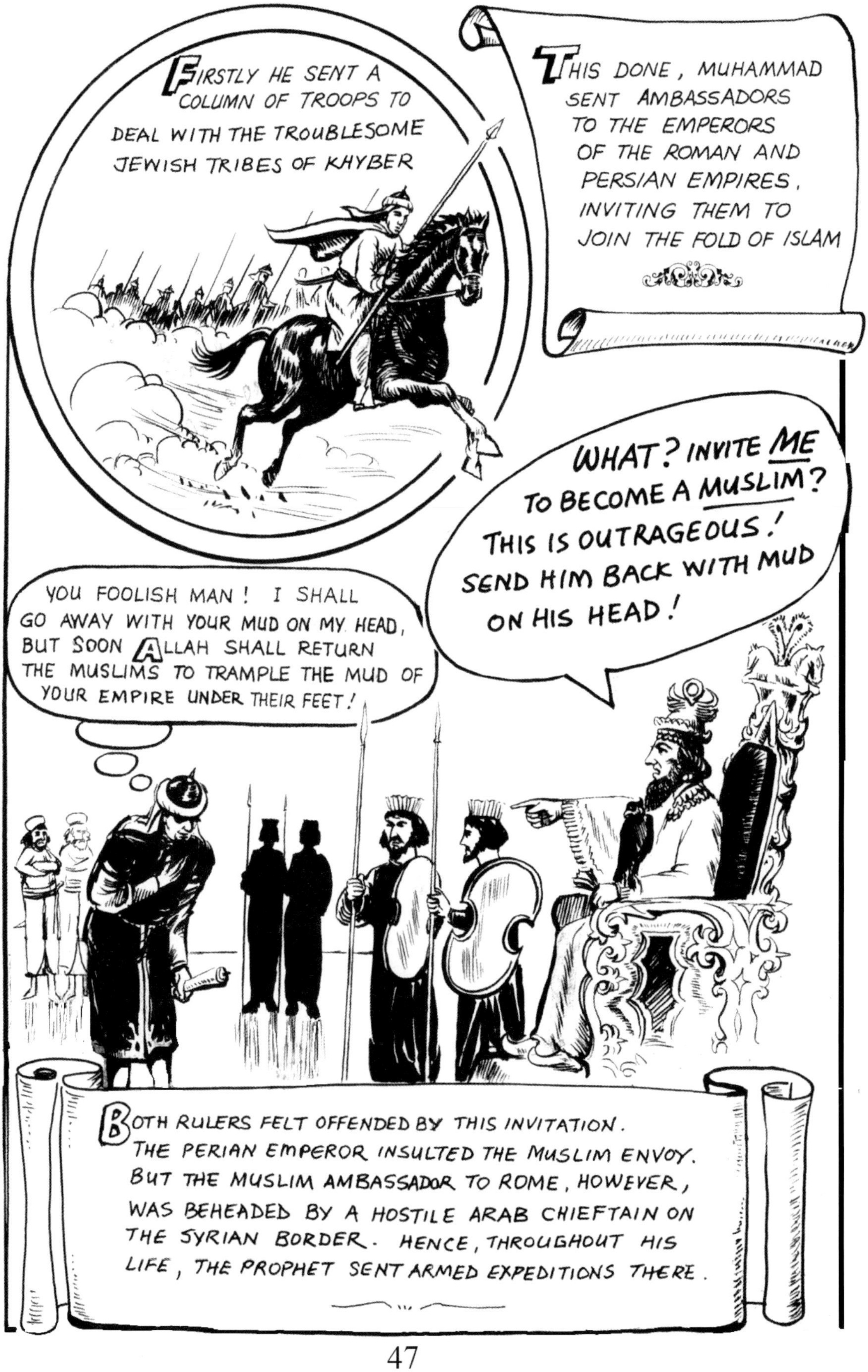
FIRSTLY HE SENT A COLUMN OF TROOPS TO DEAL WITH THE TROUBLESOME JEWISH TRIBES OF KHYBER
THIS DONE, MUHAMMAD SENT AMBASSADORS TO THE EMPERORS OF THE ROMAN AND PERSIAN EMPIRES, INVITING THEM TO JOIN THE FOLD OF ISLAM
WHAT? INVITE ME TO BECOME A MUSLIM? THIS IS OUTRAGEOUS! SEND HIM BACK WITH MUD ON HIS HEAD!
YOU FOOLISH MAN! I SHALL GO AWAY WITH YOUR MUD ON MY HEAD, BUT SOON ALLAH SHALL RETURN THE MUSLIMS TO TRAMPLE THE MUD OF YOUR EMPIRE UNDER THEIR FEET!
BOTH RULERS FELT OFFENDED BY THIS INVITATION. THE PERIAN EMPEROR INSULTED THE MUSLIM ENVOY. BUT THE MUSLIM AMBASSADOR TO ROME, HOWEVER, WAS BEHEADED BY A HOSTILE ARAB CHIEFTAIN ON THE SYRIAN BORDER. HENCE, THROUGHOUT HIS LIFE, THE PROPHET SENT ARMED EXPEDITIONS THERE.

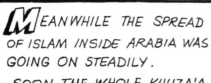MEANWHILE THE SPREAD OF ISLAM INSIDE ARABIA WAS GOING ON STEADILY.
SOON THE WHOLE KHUZA'A TRIBE HAD COME FORWARD TO JOIN THE FAITH.

I AM VERY PROUD TO BE A MUSLIM, TO BE PART OF A BIG-HEARTED NATION INSTEAD OF A SMALL, SELFISH TRIBE!

THEIR ARCH-ENEMIES, THE BANU BAKR ON THE OTHER HAND, SIDED WITH THE QURAISH.
THE BANU BAKR THEN MASSACRED A NUMBER OF BANU KHUZA'A WHO LIVED NEAR MECCA.

BUT SOON IT BECAME AN OPEN SECRET THAT THE QURAISH HAD ACTIVELY PARTICIPATED IN THE BATTLE. THIS WAS A TREACHEROUS BREACH OF THE PROMISES THEY MADE AT HUDAIBIYA. MUHAMMAD'S JUDGEMENT WAS CLEAR, RAPID AND DECISIVE...

JIHAD, JIHAD! PREPARE FOR JIHAD!

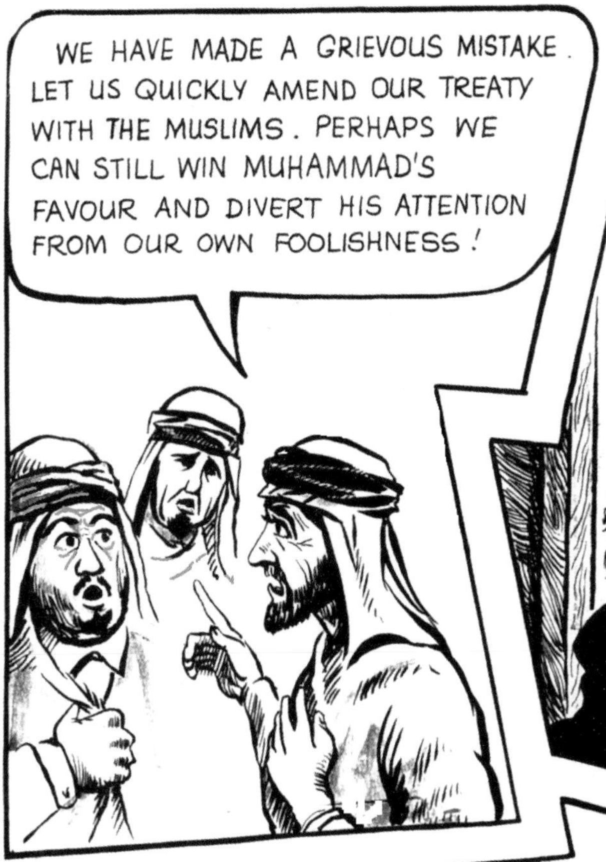
WE HAVE MADE A GRIEVOUS MISTAKE. LET US QUICKLY AMEND OUR TREATY WITH THE MUSLIMS. PERHAPS WE CAN STILL WIN MUHAMMAD'S FAVOUR AND DIVERT HIS ATTENTION FROM OUR OWN FOOLISHNESS!

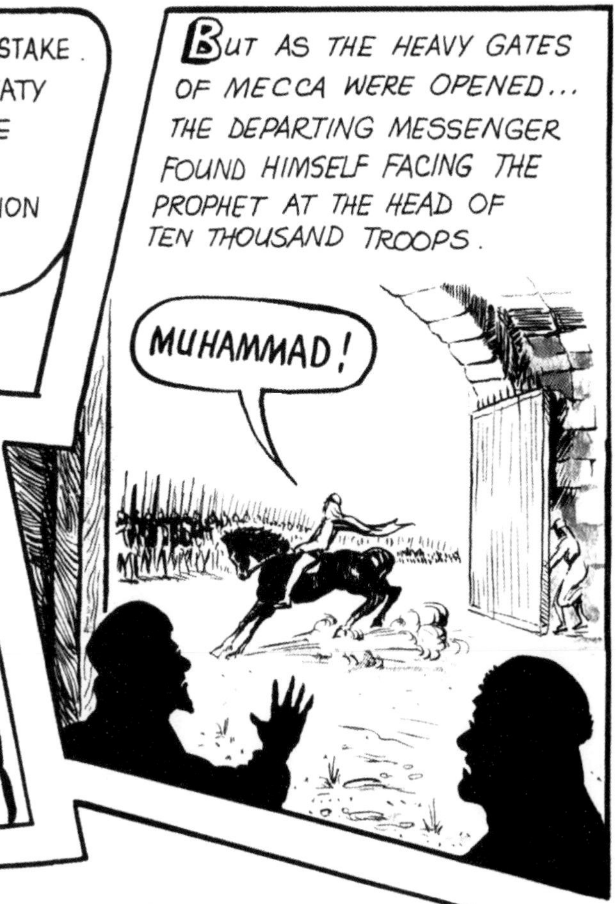
BUT AS THE HEAVY GATES OF MECCA WERE OPENED... THE DEPARTING MESSENGER FOUND HIMSELF FACING THE PROPHET AT THE HEAD OF TEN THOUSAND TROOPS.
MUHAMMAD!

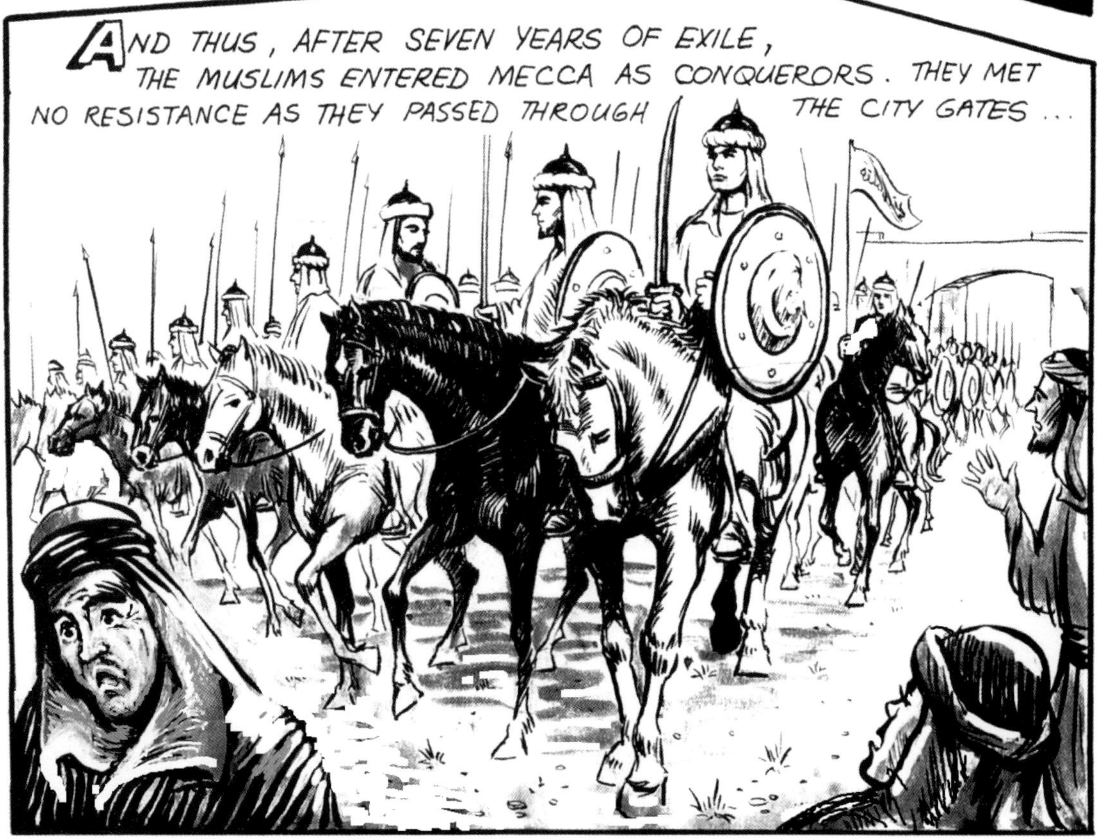
AND THUS, AFTER SEVEN YEARS OF EXILE, THE MUSLIMS ENTERED MECCA AS CONQUERORS. THEY MET NO RESISTANCE AS THEY PASSED THROUGH THE CITY GATES...

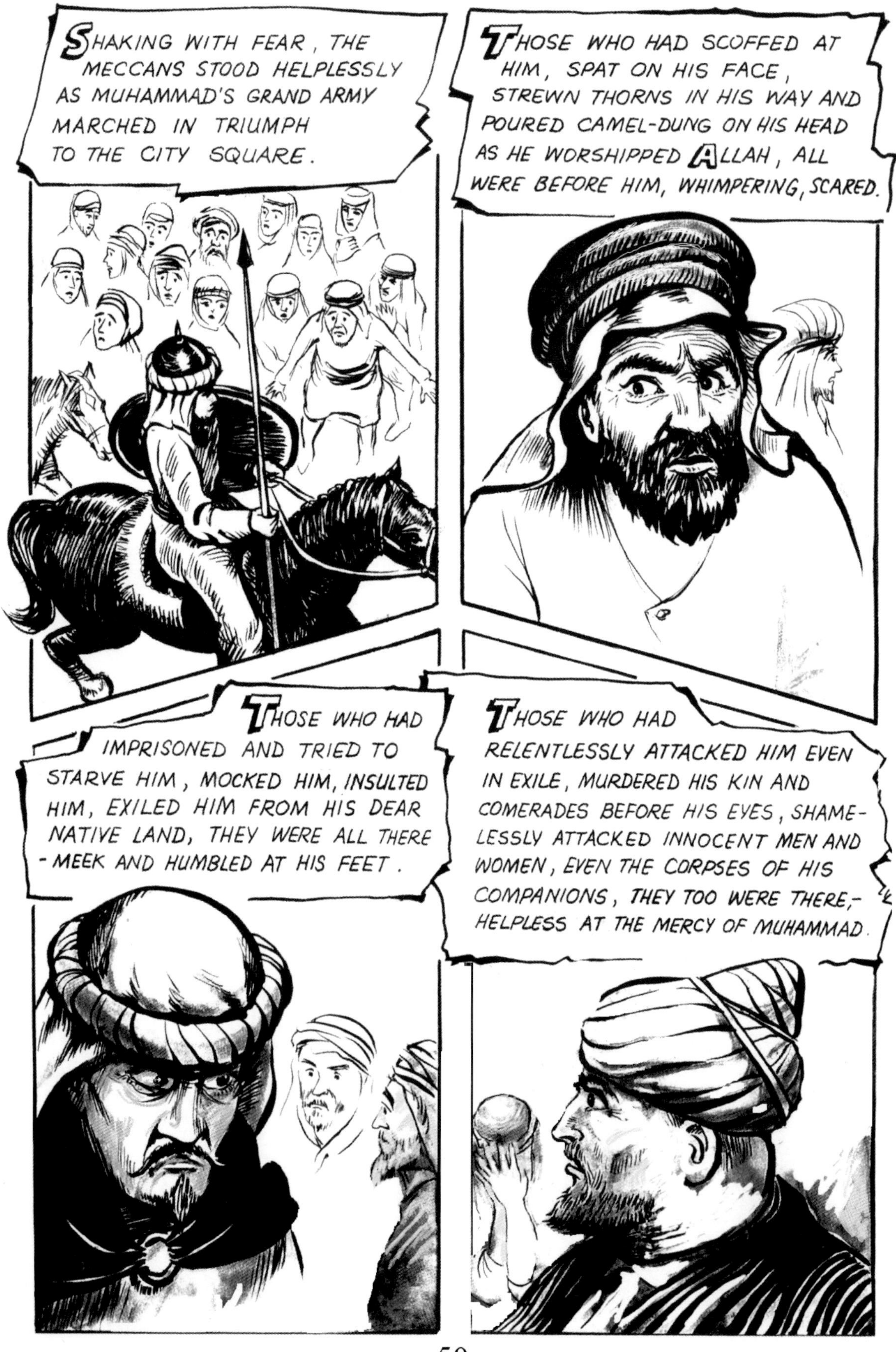
SHAKING WITH FEAR, THE MECCANS STOOD HELPLESSLY AS MUHAMMAD'S GRAND ARMY MARCHED IN TRIUMPH TO THE CITY SQUARE.
THOSE WHO HAD SCOFFED AT HIM, SPAT ON HIS FACE, STREWN THORNS IN HIS WAY AND POURED CAMEL-DUNG ON HIS HEAD AS HE WORSHIPPED ALLAH, ALL WERE BEFORE HIM, WHIMPERING, SCARED.
THOSE WHO HAD IMPRISONED AND TRIED TO STARVE HIM, MOCKED HIM, INSULTED HIM, EXILED HIM FROM HIS DEAR NATIVE LAND, THEY WERE ALL THERE - MEEK AND HUMBLED AT HIS FEET.
THOSE WHO HAD RELENTLESSLY ATTACKED HIM EVEN IN EXILE, MURDERED HIS KIN AND COMERADES BEFORE HIS EYES, SHAMELESSLY ATTACKED INNOCENT MEN AND WOMEN, EVEN THE CORPSES OF HIS COMPANIONS, THEY TOO WERE THERE,- HELPLESS AT THE MERCY OF MUHAMMAD.

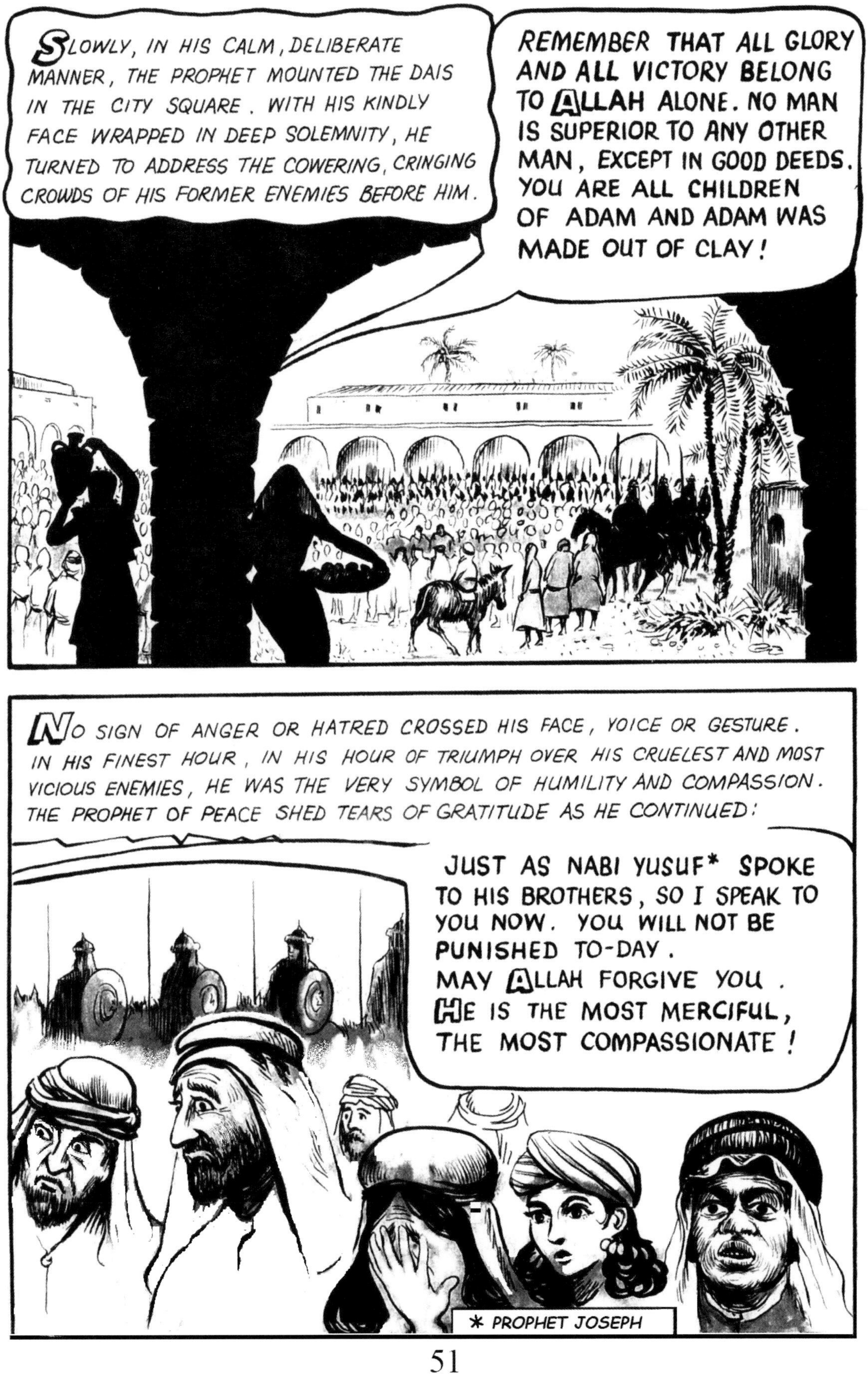
SLOWLY, IN HIS CALM, DELIBERATE MANNER, THE PROPHET MOUNTED THE DAIS IN THE CITY SQUARE. WITH HIS KINDLY FACE WRAPPED IN DEEP SOLEMNITY, HE TURNED TO ADDRESS THE COWERING, CRINGING CROWDS OF HIS FORMER ENEMIES BEFORE HIM.
REMEMBER THAT ALL GLORY AND ALL VICTORY BELONG TO ALLAH ALONE. NO MAN IS SUPERIOR TO ANY OTHER MAN, EXCEPT IN GOOD DEEDS. YOU ARE ALL CHILDREN OF ADAM AND ADAM WAS MADE OUT OF CLAY!
NO SIGN OF ANGER OR HATRED CROSSED HIS FACE, VOICE OR GESTURE. IN HIS FINEST HOUR, IN HIS HOUR OF TRIUMPH OVER HIS CRUELEST AND MOST VICIOUS ENEMIES, HE WAS THE VERY SYMBOL OF HUMILITY AND COMPASSION. THE PROPHET OF PEACE SHED TEARS OF GRATITUDE AS HE CONTINUED:
JUST AS NABI YUSUF* SPOKE TO HIS BROTHERS, SO I SPEAK TO YOU NOW. YOU WILL NOT BE PUNISHED TO-DAY. MAY ALLAH FORGIVE YOU. HE IS THE MOST MERCIFUL, THE MOST COMPASSIONATE!
* PROPHET JOSEPH

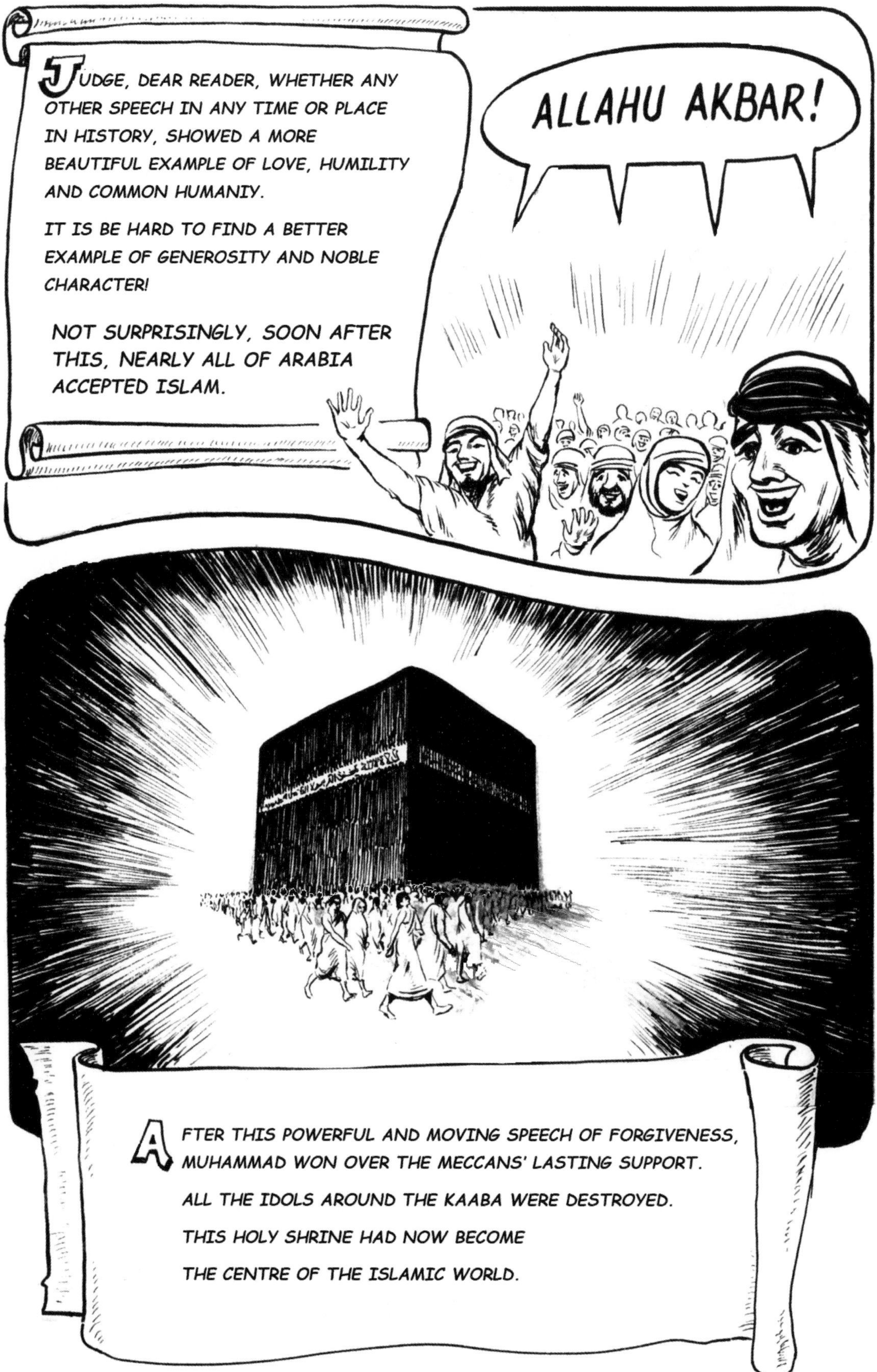
JUDGE, DEAR READER, WHETHER ANY OTHER SPEECH IN ANY TIME OR PLACE IN HISTORY, SHOWED A MORE BEAUTIFUL EXAMPLE OF LOVE, HUMILITY AND COMMON HUMANIY.
IT IS BE HARD TO FIND A BETTER EXAMPLE OF GENEROSITY AND NOBLE CHARACTER!
NOT SURPRISINGLY, SOON AFTER THIS, NEARLY ALL OF ARABIA ACCEPTED ISLAM.
ALLAHU AKBAR!
AFTER THIS POWERFUL AND MOVING SPEECH OF FORGIVENESS, MUHAMMAD WON OVER THE MECCANS' LASTING SUPPORT.
ALL THE IDOLS AROUND THE KAABA WERE DESTROYED.
THIS HOLY SHRINE HAD NOW BECOME
THE CENTRE OF THE ISLAMIC WORLD.

CHAPTER SEVEN:
The Unification of Arabia

THE POWERFUL AND RESPECTED QURAISH HAVING ACCEPTED ISLAM, IT WAS NOT LONG BEFORE WHOLE TRIBES FROM FAR-FLUNG CORNERS OF ARABIA JOINED THE MUSLIMS.

BY THE YEAR 9 A.H. (631 A.C.) VARIOUS FOREIGN EMBASSIES HAD BEEN ESTABLISHED IN MECCA. THE HOLY PROPHET NOW GOVERNED ARABIA BY THE LAWS OF ISLAM. STATE-CONTROLLED ZAKAAT (POOR-TAX) WAS STARTED. RELIGIOUS UNITY JOINED ALL THE TRIBES INTO A SINGLE NATION (UMMAH).

THE UNIFICATION OF ARABIA WAS PROCEEDING STEADILY AND SOON THE LANDS OF ISLAM STRETCHED FROM THE PERSIAN GULF TO THE RED SEA, AND FROM YEMEN IN THE SOUTH TO THE BORDERS OF SYRIA IN THE NORTH.

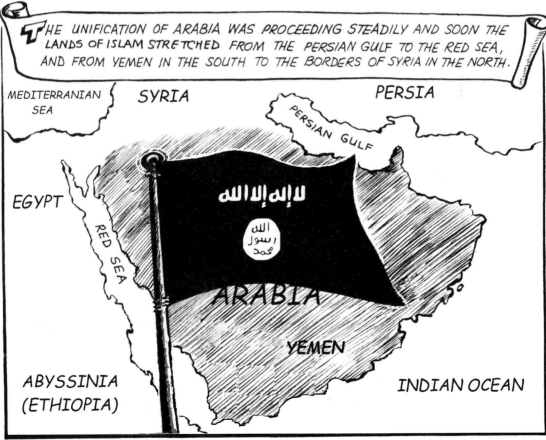

MEDITERRANIAN SEA
SYRIA
PERSIA
PERSIAN GULF
EGYPT
RED SEA
لا إله إلا الله
الله
رسول
محمد
ARABIA
YEMEN
ABYSSINIA (ETHIOPIA)
INDIAN OCEAN

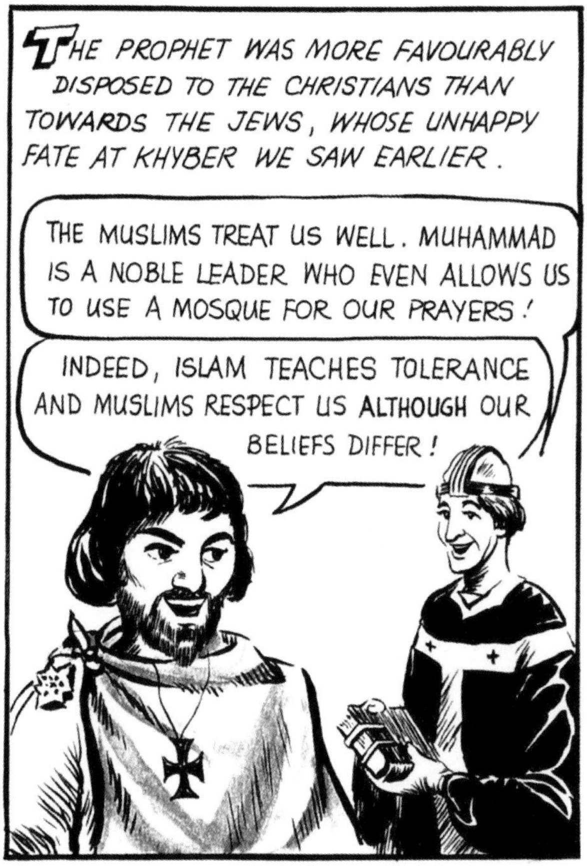
THE PROPHET WAS MORE FAVOURABLY DISPOSED TO THE CHRISTIANS THAN TOWARDS THE JEWS, WHOSE UNHAPPY FATE AT KHYBER WE SAW EARLIER.
THE MUSLIMS TREAT US WELL. MUHAMMAD IS A NOBLE LEADER WHO EVEN ALLOWS US TO USE A MOSQUE FOR OUR PRAYERS!
INDEED, ISLAM TEACHES TOLERANCE AND MUSLIMS RESPECT US ALTHOUGH OUR BELIEFS DIFFER!

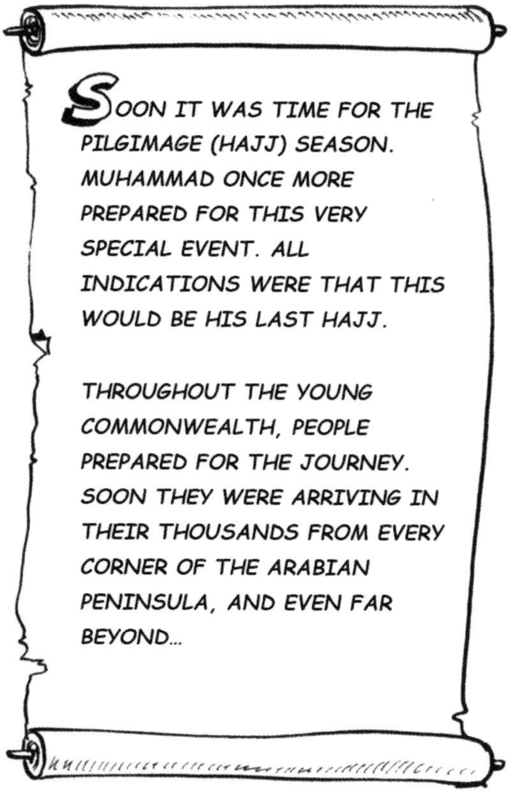
SOON IT WAS TIME FOR THE PILGIMAGE (HAJJ) SEASON. MUHAMMAD ONCE MORE PREPARED FOR THIS VERY SPECIAL EVENT. ALL INDICATIONS WERE THAT THIS WOULD BE HIS LAST HAJJ.
THROUGHOUT THE YOUNG COMMONWEALTH, PEOPLE PREPARED FOR THE JOURNEY. SOON THEY WERE ARRIVING IN THEIR THOUSANDS FROM EVERY CORNER OF THE ARABIAN PENINSULA, AND EVEN FAR BEYOND...

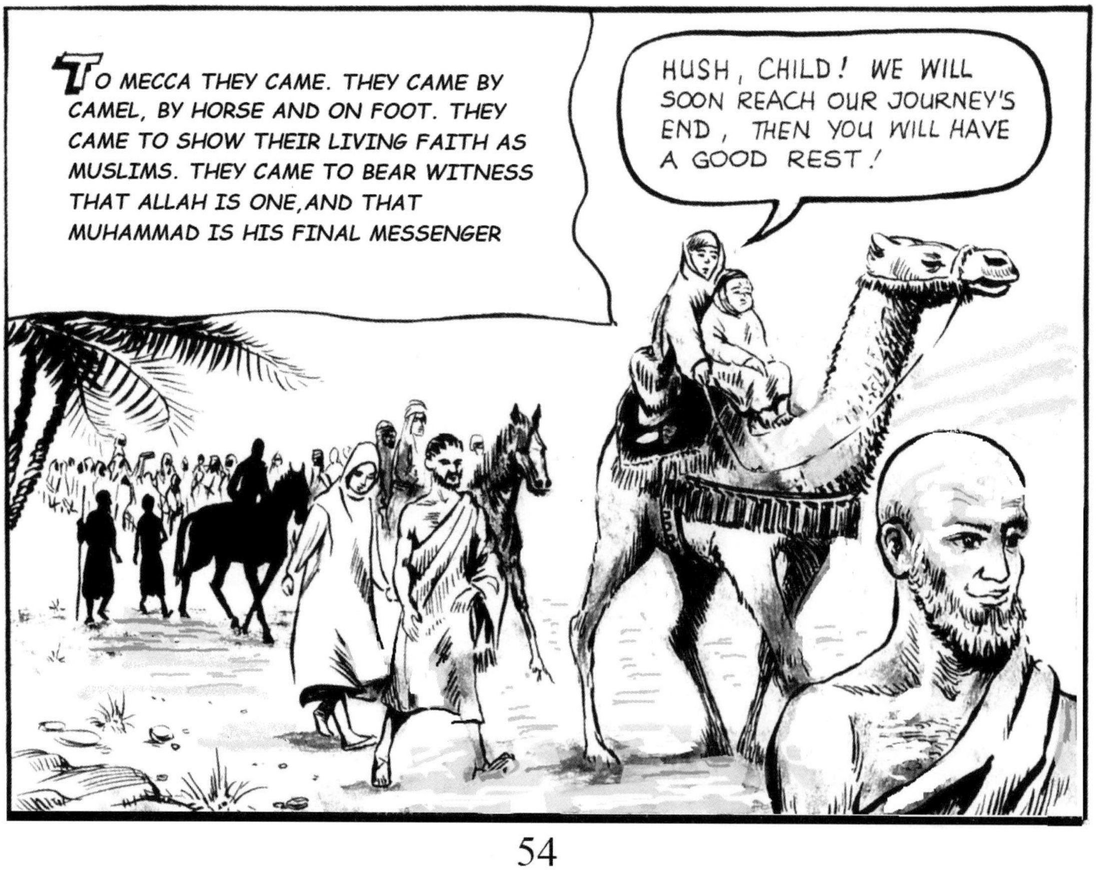
TO MECCA THEY CAME. THEY CAME BY CAMEL, BY HORSE AND ON FOOT. THEY CAME TO SHOW THEIR LIVING FAITH AS MUSLIMS. THEY CAME TO BEAR WITNESS THAT ALLAH IS ONE,AND THAT MUHAMMAD IS HIS FINAL MESSENGER
HUSH, CHILD! WE WILL SOON REACH OUR JOURNEY'S END, THEN YOU WILL HAVE A GOOD REST!

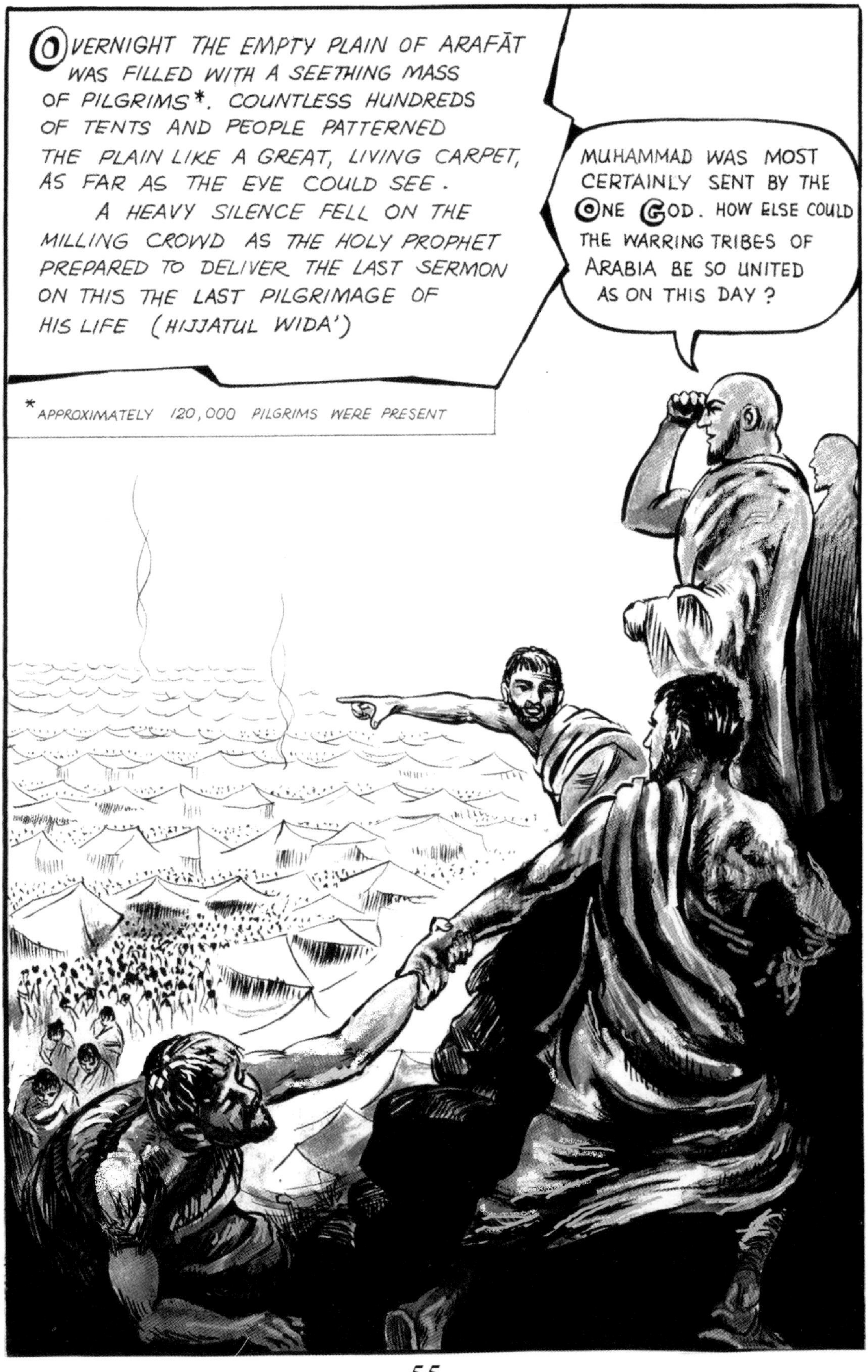
OVERNIGHT THE EMPTY PLAIN OF ARAFĀT WAS FILLED WITH A SEETHING MASS OF PILGRIMS*. COUNTLESS HUNDREDS OF TENTS AND PEOPLE PATTERNED THE PLAIN LIKE A GREAT, LIVING CARPET, AS FAR AS THE EYE COULD SEE.
A HEAVY SILENCE FELL ON THE MILLING CROWD AS THE HOLY PROPHET PREPARED TO DELIVER THE LAST SERMON ON THIS THE LAST PILGRIMAGE OF HIS LIFE (HIJJATUL WIDA')
*APPROXIMATELY 120,000 PILGRIMS WERE PRESENT
MUHAMMAD WAS MOST CERTAINLY SENT BY THE ONE GOD. HOW ELSE COULD THE WARRING TRIBES OF ARABIA BE SO UNITED AS ON THIS DAY?

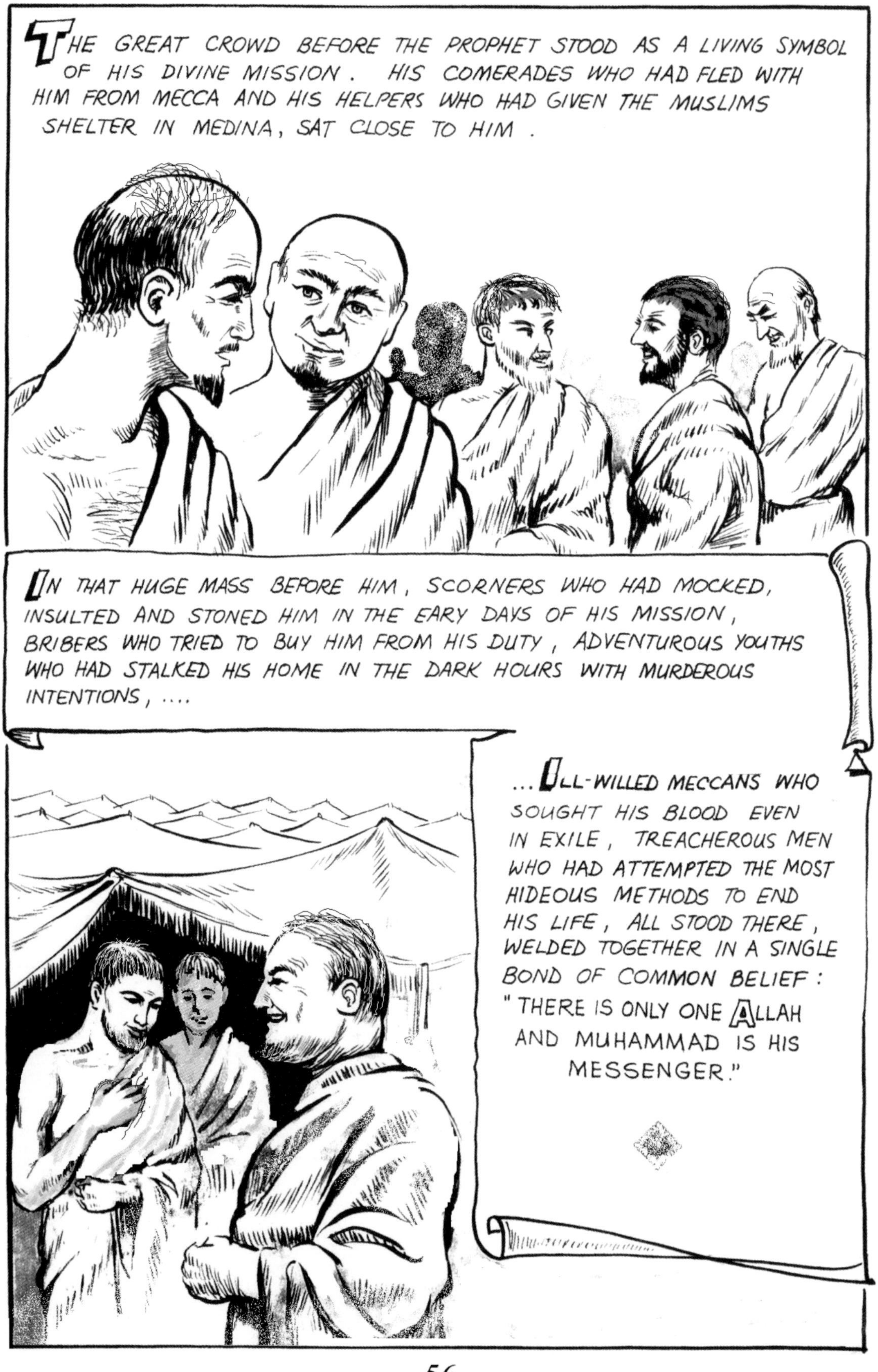
THE GREAT CROWD BEFORE THE PROPHET STOOD AS A LIVING SYMBOL OF HIS DIVINE MISSION. HIS COMERADES WHO HAD FLED WITH HIM FROM MECCA AND HIS HELPERS WHO HAD GIVEN THE MUSLIMS SHELTER IN MEDINA, SAT CLOSE TO HIM.
IN THAT HUGE MASS BEFORE HIM, SCORNERS WHO HAD MOCKED, INSULTED AND STONED HIM IN THE EARY DAYS OF HIS MISSION, BRIBERS WHO TRIED TO BUY HIM FROM HIS DUTY, ADVENTUROUS YOUTHS WHO HAD STALKED HIS HOME IN THE DARK HOURS WITH MURDEROUS INTENTIONS, ...
... ILL-WILLED MECCANS WHO SOUGHT HIS BLOOD EVEN IN EXILE, TREACHEROUS MEN WHO HAD ATTEMPTED THE MOST HIDEOUS METHODS TO END HIS LIFE, ALL STOOD THERE, WELDED TOGETHER IN A SINGLE BOND OF COMMON BELIEF: "THERE IS ONLY ONE ALLAH AND MUHAMMAD IS HIS MESSENGER."

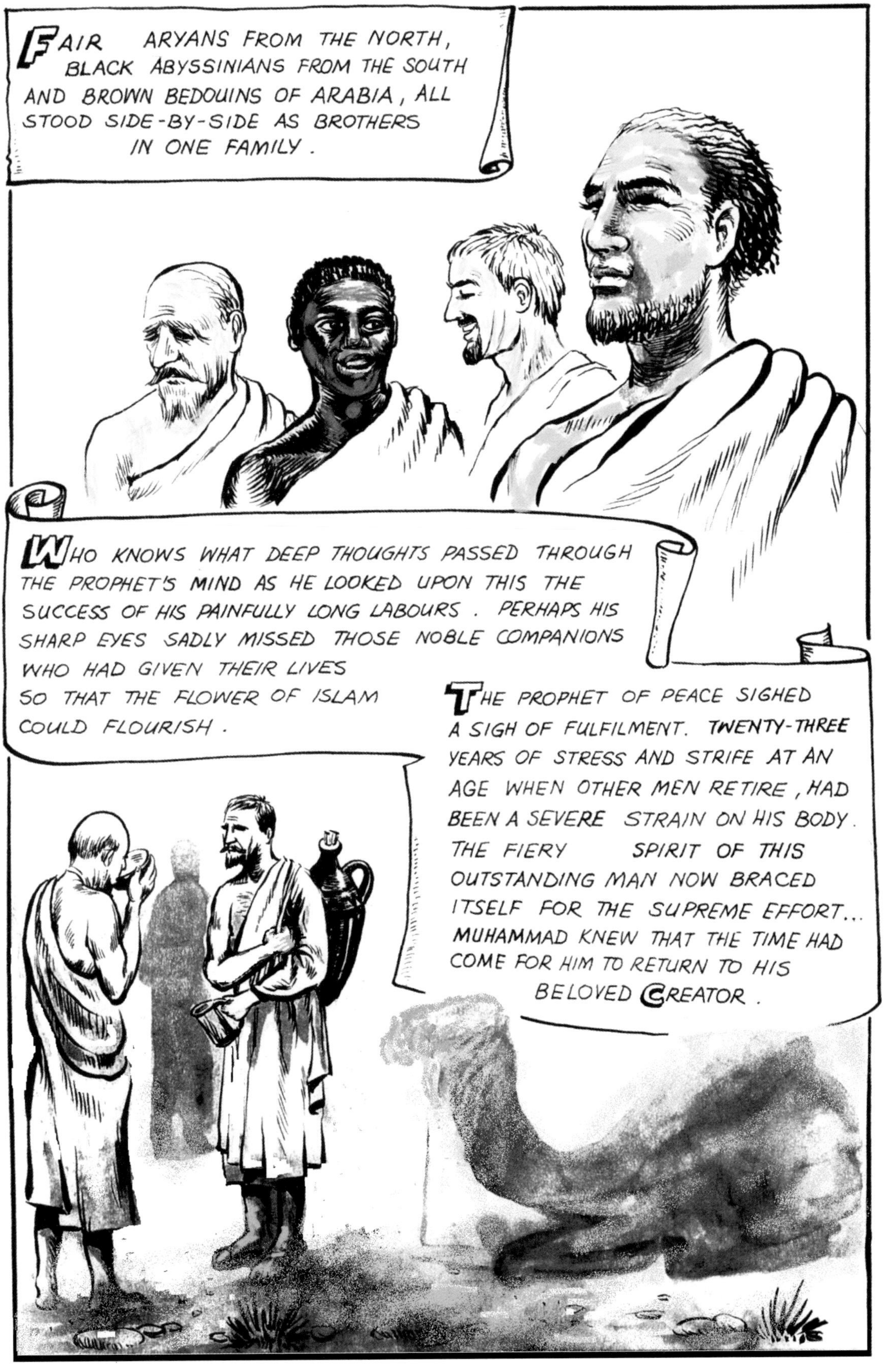
FAIR ARYANS FROM THE NORTH, BLACK ABYSSINIANS FROM THE SOUTH AND BROWN BEDOUINS OF ARABIA, ALL STOOD SIDE-BY-SIDE AS BROTHERS IN ONE FAMILY.
WHO KNOWS WHAT DEEP THOUGHTS PASSED THROUGH THE PROPHET'S MIND AS HE LOOKED UPON THIS THE SUCCESS OF HIS PAINFULLY LONG LABOURS. PERHAPS HIS SHARP EYES SADLY MISSED THOSE NOBLE COMPANIONS WHO HAD GIVEN THEIR LIVES SO THAT THE FLOWER OF ISLAM COULD FLOURISH.
THE PROPHET OF PEACE SIGHED A SIGH OF FULFILMENT. TWENTY-THREE YEARS OF STRESS AND STRIFE AT AN AGE WHEN OTHER MEN RETIRE, HAD BEEN A SEVERE STRAIN ON HIS BODY. THE FIERY SPIRIT OF THIS OUTSTANDING MAN NOW BRACED ITSELF FOR THE SUPREME EFFORT... MUHAMMAD KNEW THAT THE TIME HAD COME FOR HIM TO RETURN TO HIS BELOVED CREATOR.

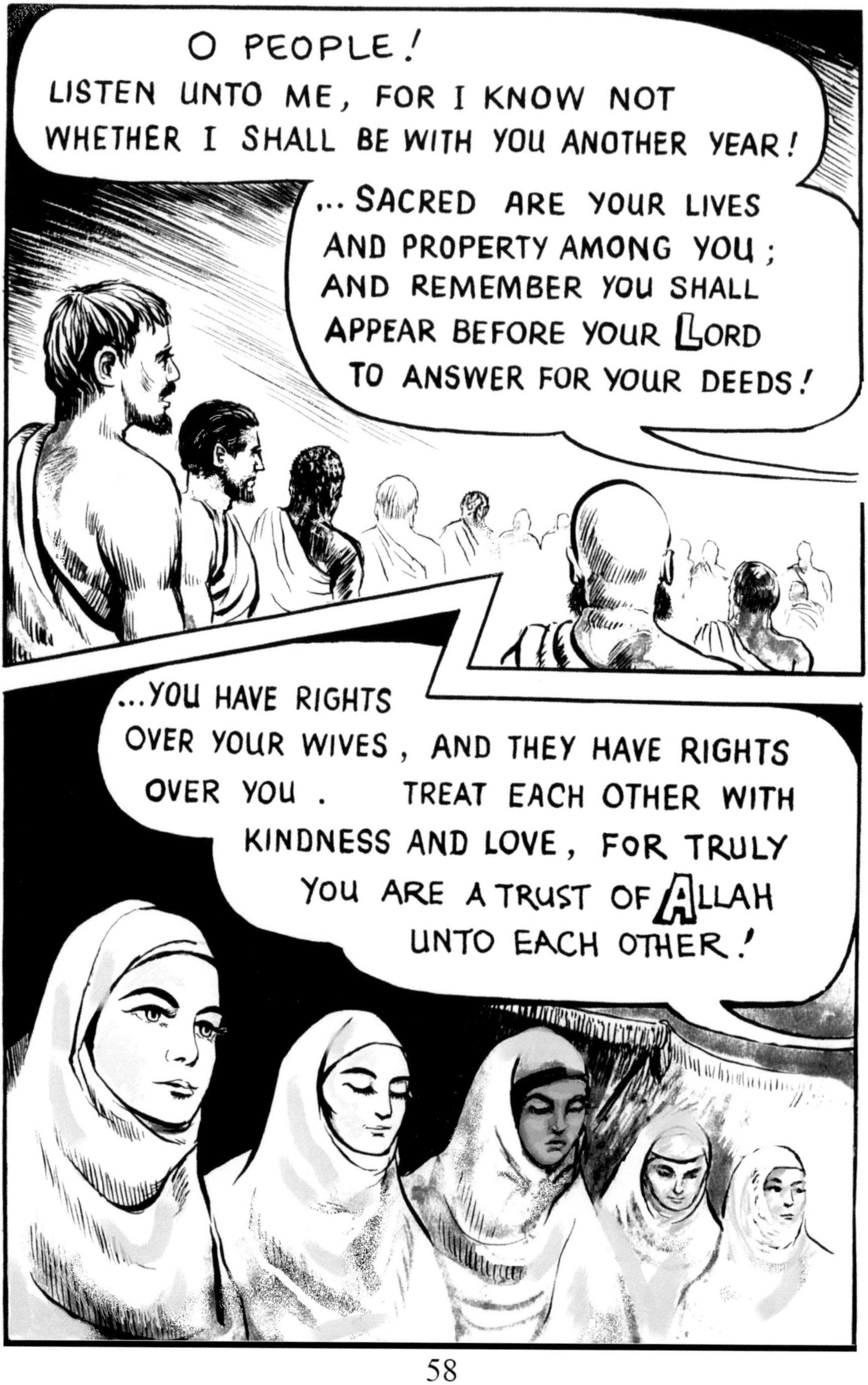
O PEOPLE! LISTEN UNTO ME, FOR I KNOW NOT WHETHER I SHALL BE WITH YOU ANOTHER YEAR!
...SACRED ARE YOUR LIVES AND PROPERTY AMONG YOU; AND REMEMBER YOU SHALL APPEAR BEFORE YOUR LORD TO ANSWER FOR YOUR DEEDS!
...YOU HAVE RIGHTS OVER YOUR WIVES, AND THEY HAVE RIGHTS OVER YOU. TREAT EACH OTHER WITH KINDNESS AND LOVE, FOR TRULY YOU ARE A TRUST OF ALLAH UNTO EACH OTHER!

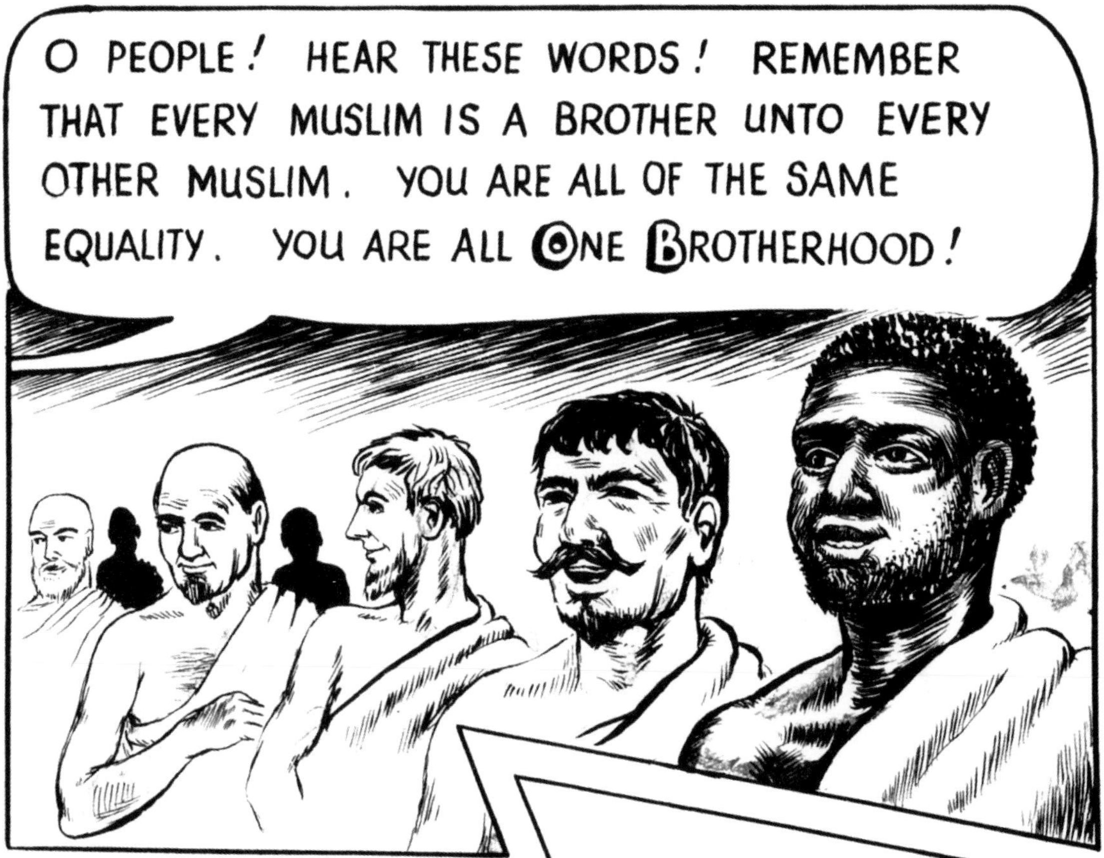
O PEOPLE! HEAR THESE WORDS! REMEMBER THAT EVERY MUSLIM IS A BROTHER UNTO EVERY OTHER MUSLIM. YOU ARE ALL OF THE SAME EQUALITY. YOU ARE ALL ONE BROTHERHOOD!

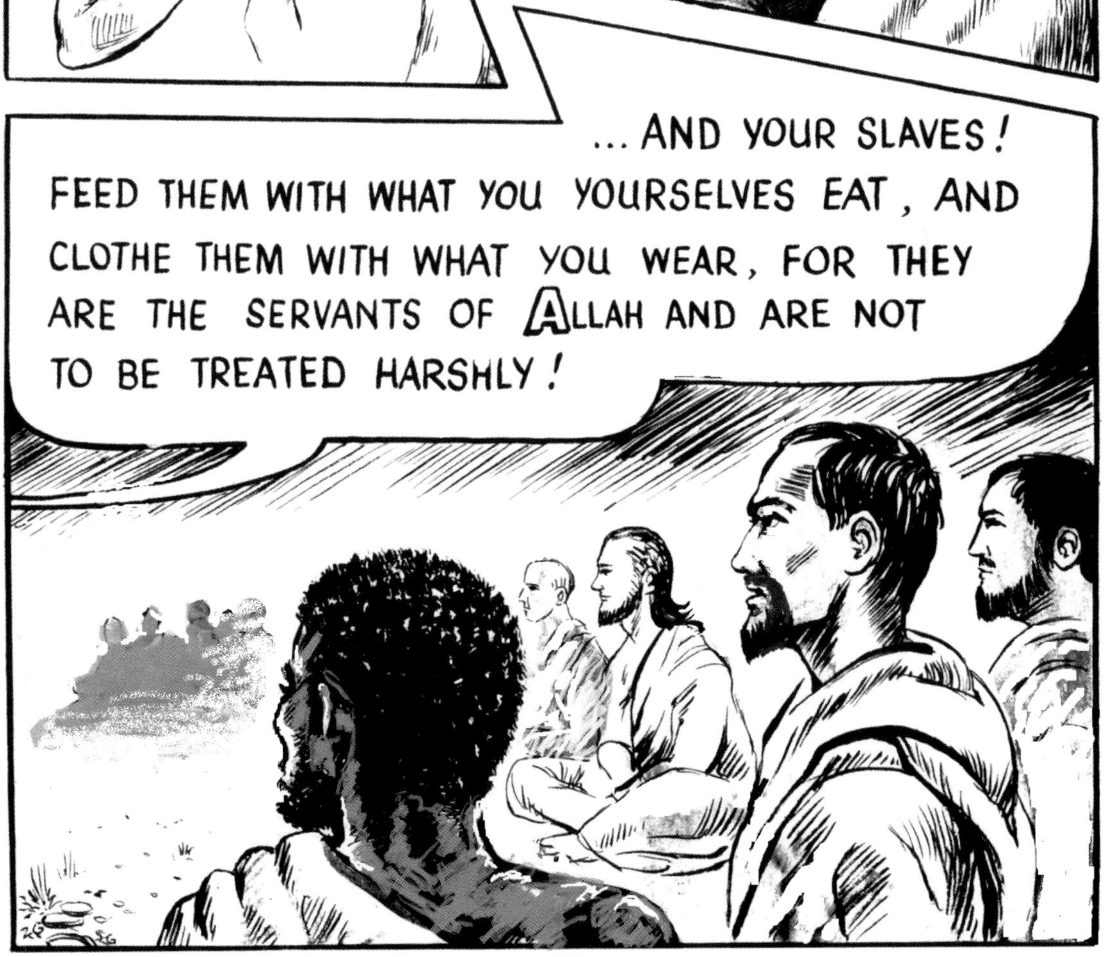
...AND YOUR SLAVES! FEED THEM WITH WHAT YOU YOURSELVES EAT, AND CLOTHE THEM WITH WHAT YOU WEAR, FOR THEY ARE THE SERVANTS OF ALLAH AND ARE NOT TO BE TREATED HARSHLY!

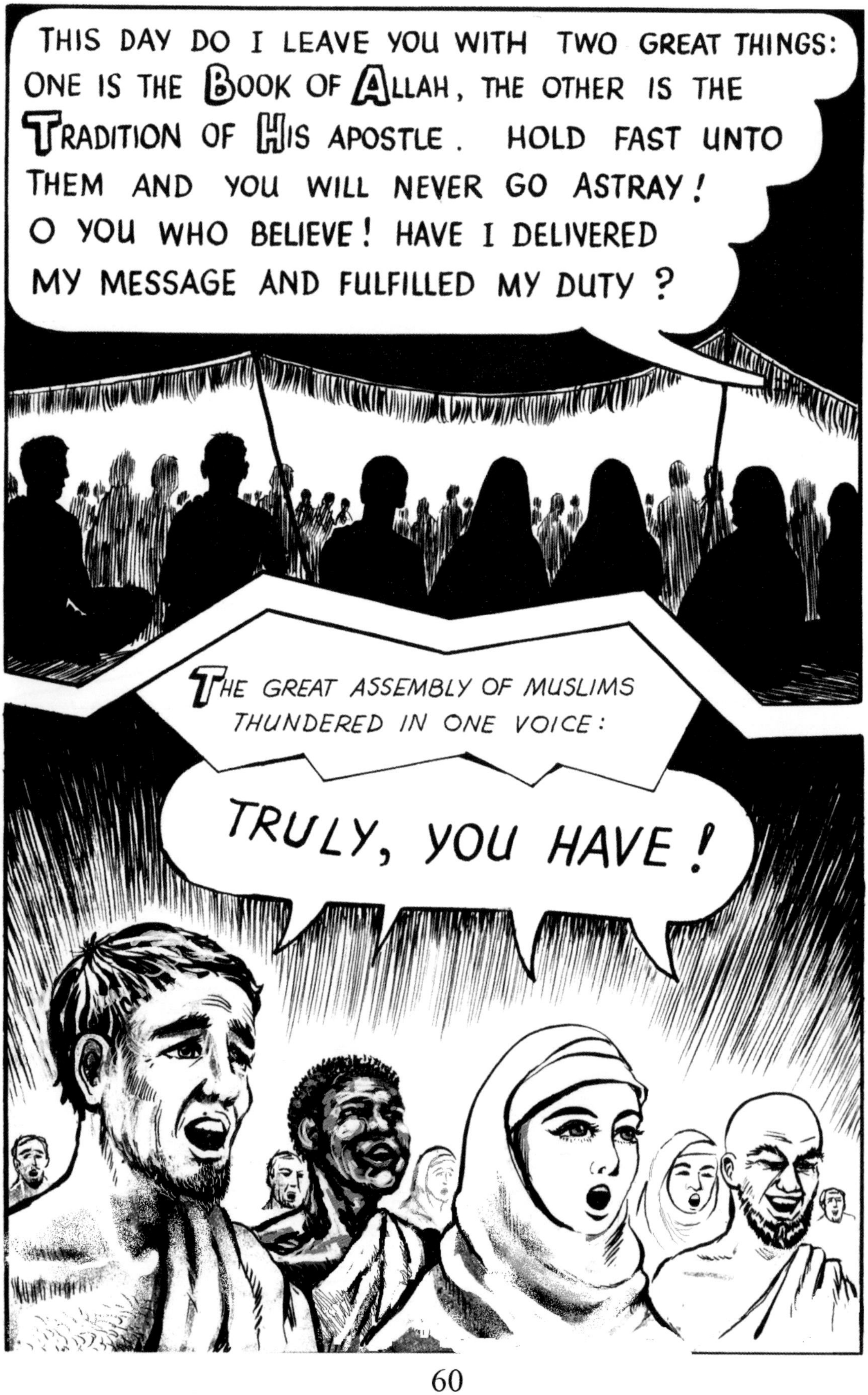
THIS DAY DO I LEAVE YOU WITH TWO GREAT THINGS: ONE IS THE BOOK OF ALLAH, THE OTHER IS THE TRADITION OF HIS APOSTLE. HOLD FAST UNTO THEM AND YOU WILL NEVER GO ASTRAY! O YOU WHO BELIEVE! HAVE I DELIVERED MY MESSAGE AND FULFILLED MY DUTY?
THE GREAT ASSEMBLY OF MUSLIMS THUNDERED IN ONE VOICE:
TRULY, YOU HAVE!

WITH HIS STRENGTH SAPPED BY AGE AND AN ACTIVE LIFE, MUHAMMAD CRIED OUT, RAISING TO THE HEAVENS THOSE HANDS WHICH HAD FASHIONED OUT OF THE DRY DUST OF ARABIA, A GREAT SPIRITUAL EMPIRE.

O ALLAH, I BEG OF YOU, BEAR WITNESS TO THIS DAY!

THE PROPHET MUHAMMAD DIED ON THE 13th RABIUL-AWWAL, 11 A.H. (8th JUNE 632 A.C.) IT IS WIDELY AGGREED BY HISTORIANS OF THAT TIME, THAT IN THE ANNALS OF WORLD HISTORY, NO POLITICAL LEADER OR SOCIAL REFORMER COMMANDED SUCH IMPLICIT OBEDIENCE FROM HIS MANY FOLLOWERS. MUHAMMAD PREDICTED THAT THE ROMAN AND PERSIAN EMPIRES WOULD BE OVER-RUN BY THE MUSLIMS. BUT THE GLORY OF MILITARY CONQUEST AND THE LURE OF MATERIAL GAINS NEVER SWAYED HIS DETERMINATION TO CARRY OUT HIS DUTY. THE PROPHET OF ISLAM ON THE EVE OF HIS PASSING SPOKE NOT OF SOVEREIGNTY NOR OF HIS MANY GLORIOUS ACHIEVEMENTS. THE SOLDIER OF TRUTH SHOT HIS LAST FEW ARROWS FROM HIS NOW EXHAUSTED BOW, DEFENDING THE RIGHTS OF THE WEAK, THE SICK, THE WIDOWS, THE ORPHANS, THE SLAVES, THE POOR, THE OPPRESSED. MUHAMMAD DIED AS HE HAD LIVED: IN THE UNSWERVING DEVOTION OF THE MAN TO THE MISSION. HIS ROUSING MESSAGE ARMED A WILD DESERT PEOPLE WITH THE TORCH OF TRUTH, TO LIGHT THE DARK AGES WITH LEARNING AND CULTURE. IT ROLLED AND THUNDERED ACROSS THE PAGES OF HISTORY, AND IS TO-DAY THE LIVING FAITH OF ONE-SEVENTH OF HUMANITY* THE HIGH STANDARD OF MORAL CONDUCT SET BY THE PROPHET OF ISLAM STILL INSPIRES THE YOUTH TO-DAY, AND OUR TROUBLED WORLD COULD LEARN MUCH FROM MUHAMMAD'S EXAMPLE.

* 1970 : Muslims approximately 15% of world population
2015 : Muslims approximately 25% of world population
(According to the Pew Research organisation)